The Fryeburg Chronicles
Book III
Portraits of Change

By June O'Donal

PRESS

In Loving Memory

To My Mother, Theresa P. Amaral
1930-2013

"It is impossible to enslave, mentally or socially, a Bible-reading people. The principles of the Bible are the groundwork of human freedom."

Horace Greeley

"You may choose to look the other way but you can never say again that you did not know."

William Wilberforce

Table of Contents

Acknowledgements

Writing is a solitary endeavor; however it takes a community to do research. I am most grateful to the patient staff at the Fryeburg Public Library who ordered numerous interlibrary loan books for me. I thank both the Fryeburg Historical Society and the Maine Historical Society for making available the many resources in their research libraries.

There are several Fryeburg residents who personally provided me with information. My thanks go to Doug and Paula Albert, the current owners of the Benjamin Wiley House for answering my questions. In addition they interviewed eighty-one year old James Record, a life- long resident of North Fryeburg, who shared valuable information which he learned from his grandmother, Grace Howard about the location and size of the secret room in this house.

I like to thank my meticulous and patient husband for drawing the graphics and maps.

About the cover: Sadie Miller painting a local landscape. The lovely front parlor is located at The Fryeburg Historical Society's new home on 83 Portland Street. The oil painted landscape is the work of artist Jon Marshall of Denmark, ME. Erica Boynton of Remick Country Doctor Museum and Farm in Tamworth, NH lent us the period costume. Lynne Schabhetl, a Bridgeton, ME resident and senior at Dean

College, posed as Sadie. Fryeburg resident and professional photographer, Betsy Marcello, shot the photo. Betsy is a direct descendant of David Evans, one of the original settlers of Fryeburg.

Chronology of Events

1792 – Fryeburg Academy is established

1806 – Fryeburg Academy's larger, two-story wooden structure is built on the present day site. Girls are admitted to attend during the summer session.

1812 – The War of 1812 – 1815

1814 – Forty-three Fryeburg men under Capt. Philip Eastman are sent to Fort Burroughs to protect Portland from a possible British invasion.
The British burn the Capitol Building and the President's House in Washington, D.C.

1816 – Construction of the Fryeburg Canal begins

1817 – Construction of the Erie Canal begins

1818 – The death of Abigail Adams

1819 – The Panic of 1819
July –   The Province of Maine votes for independence from Massachusetts
October – Maine state constitution is written in Portland

1820 – The publication of Washington Irving's Sketch Book
March–Maine becomes the 23rd state

1825 – The Centennial celebration of Lovewell's Fight
on the northern shore of Saco Pond, now called
Lovewell's Pond

1826 – July 4 – The 50th anniversary of the Declaration of
Independence
The death of John Adams
August–The Crawford Notch Landslide kills the
Willey family

Miller Family Tree

I. **James Miller and Sarah Bradford Miller**
  A. **Micah Miller** born 1764 married Grace Peabody in 1785
     1. Elizabeth (Libby) Peabody Miller born 1786 married Edward Endicott of Boston. (Had four children.)
     2. Sarah (Sadie) Alden Miller born 1788
     3. William Peabody Miller born 1792, died 1792
     4. Alden James Miller born 1794
  B. **Benjamin James Miller** born 1767 married Hannah Chase in 1793
     1. Jacob Freeman Miller born 1794 married Katherine Wiley in 1813
        a. Elijah James Miller born 1814
        b. Daniel Chase Miller born 1816
     2. Abigail Bradford Miller born 1796
  C. **Abigail Elizabeth Miller** born 1767 died 1780
  D. **Ethan Jacob Miller** born 1769 married Olivia Edwards of Williamsburg, Virginia in 1802.
     1. Stepdaughter Margaret (Maggie) Edwards
     2. Matthew James Miller born 1802
     3. Mark Bradford Miller born 1804
     4. Luke Ethan Miller born 1806
     5. John Benjamin Miller born 1808
     6. Asher James Miller born 1814

Cast of Characters

Town's People:

Judah Dana – is the inspiration for Benjamin Miller. He was the first attorney in Oxford County arriving in Fryeburg in 1798. He served as District Attorney for Oxford County 1805 – 1811, Judge of Probate 1811 – 1822, a delegate to the convention that framed the state constitution of Maine and briefly served as a United States Senator of Maine. His elegant, white house stood on the corner of Main Street and River Street from 1816 through 1956.

Simon Frye – the nephew of founder Joseph Frye, was also one of the original settlers of the town and petitioners to the Commonwealth of Massachusetts for the Fryeburg Academy Grant in 1792. He settled in the eastern end of the Menotomy district near the Saco River where he ran a ferry.

Reverend Carlton Hurd – served as pastor to the Second Parish Church also called the South Meeting House in the Village from 1823 – 1855. He was held in high esteem holding a Doctor of Divinity from Dartmouth College. It was under his leadership that the current Congregational Church on Main Street was built in 1848.

Limbo – was born a free man in Guinea, Africa and captured by slave traders while he was out feeding silk worms. Little is known about his early life or arrival to America. He was a slave of William McClellan of Gorham in the District of Maine. He spent the winter of 1762-63 watching cattle in Pequawket, before the first settlement of the Seven Lots in Fryeburg. He ran away from his master and ended up the slave of Moses Ames in Fryeburg. Tradition tells that Samuel Osgood, the patriarch of the Osgood clan, bought Limbo for a yoke of oxen. In 1790 Samuel sold Limbo to his son James for 5 shillings. He died at the age of ninety in 1828 and is buried at the Village Cemetery. There is no historical evidence that he was literate or part of the Underground Railroad.

Mrs. James (Abigail) Osgood – was the daughter-in-law of Samuel Osgood and the widow of Lt. James Osgood. Affectionately called "Aunt Nabby" she owned Limbo and cared for him during his last years. Upon the death of her husband she ran the Oxford House for many years before selling it to Phillip C. Johnson.

Rufus Porter – attended the newly established Fryeburg Academy when it was a one room school house. An artist and inventor, he became well known for painting landscapes and landscape murals in homes and taverns. He was the inspiration for Sadie Miller.

Deacon Sanborn – one of the first settlers in East Fryeburg, his farm house was located between the old course of the Saco and Kezar Pond.

Mr. and Mrs. Ephraim Weston – arrived in Fryeburg in 1799 with their family and purchased 46 acres of farmland from Captain Henry Young Brown. Today Weston's Farm and Market, a thriving business and local landmark, is still in the Weston Family.

Benjamin Wiley – one of the early settlers of Fryeburg and a large landowner in North Fryeburg he built the original house in 1772 and constructed additions and barns in 1790- 1792. He was a founder of the local Universalist Church Society and one of the soldiers from Fryeburg sent to protect the residents of Bethel after it was raided by Indians in August 1781. His home still stands on Fish Street by the old course of the Saco River.

International Figures:

Abigail Adams – Patriot and wife of John Adams, the second President of the United States.

John Adams – Patriot, member of the Continental Congress, he served two terms as George Washington's Vice-President and one term as the second President of the United States.

John Quincy Adams – Son of John and Abigail Adams he was elected as the sixth President of the United States in the controversial election of 1824.

E.I. DuPont – A French immigrant, who settled in Delaware, invented a more powerful gun powder called black powder. This powder was essential in blowing up solid rock in order to build the Erie Canal.

Washington Irving – One of the first internationally known American authors, his *Sketch Book* includes the short stories of Rip Van Winkle and The Legend of Sleepy Hollow.

Andrew Jackson – A national hero after the Battle of New Orleans in the War 1812, he lost his first bid for the Presidency in 1824 running against John Quincy Adams. He was elected in 1828 as the seventh President of the United States.

Francis Cabot Lowell – While visiting England he memorized the workings of British spinning and weaving machines operated by water power. He built the successful Boston Manufacturing Company, a cotton textile mill, in Waltham by the Charles River. After his death, his business partners expanded the enterprise on the Merrimack River and named the new mill town Lowell.

Charles Spurgeon – This 19th Century British Baptist minister was dubbed "Prince of Preachers". He was a prolific author of books, sermons, commentaries, devotionals etc. Excerpts from one of his Christmas sermons were quoted.

Booker T. Washington – Born into slavery, he was emancipated at the close of the Civil War. After receiving an education, he was hired as the leader of a new all-black state school, The Tuskegee Institute, dedicated to educating and providing self-help skills to the newly freed slaves. The Tuskegee Institute was my inspiration for Hannah's Freedmen's School.

Noah Webster – A lexicographer and textbook pioneer, his blue-back speller taught generations how to read and spell. He is best known for Webster's American Dictionary of the English Language.

Canvass White – visited canals in England to study their locks. His information helped the Erie Canal planners design 83 locks, each 90 feet long, 15 feet wide and 8 feet and 4 inches high.

William Wilberforce – A deeply religious member of the English Parliament and a social reformer, he was very influential in the abolition of the slave trade and eventually slavery itself in the British Empire.

I

The Funeral

The Congregational Church in Fryeburg Village was filled beyond capacity; the over flowing crowd spilled out through the open doors and down the front steps. A warm summer breeze gently blew through the opened windows. A white pine casket and a bouquet of fragrant lilacs lay in front of the church.

Reverend Carlton Hurd climbed the steps to the pulpit high above the congregation. After the death of the beloved Reverend William Fessenden in 1805, a series of short-term pastors passed through town. Reverend Hurd promised himself that ministering to this humble body of believers would be his life's work.[1]

On June 14, 1819 Fryeburg lost one of its finest citizens, an early settler, a prominent farmer, selectman, church elder and friend to all."

Most of the original homesteaders of this small town carved out of the wilderness by the Saco River were dead. General Joseph Frye, who founded the town, was granted the land by King George III in 1763 for his services in the French and Indian War. Lt. Caleb Swan, a Harvard graduate and a classmate of President John Adams, married Joseph Frye's sister, Dorothy and settled on a parcel of land by the river now called Swan's Falls. Samuel Osgood, who built the first framed house in the village, fathered ten children and was the patriarch of the Osgood clan. His eldest son, Lt. James Osgood built and ran the Oxford House. Moses Ames was a prominent citizen who served as the first post master and one of the original trustees of Fryeburg Academy. Jonathan Dresser, known as the friend to the Indians, often hosted as many as twenty Indians in his kitchen. Brothers John and David Evans settled on the shore of Lovewell's Pond and founded the first harness and saddler shop in the village. They too were gone.[2]

"More importantly, James Miller was a humble man of God. He was a husband who loved and cherished his wife of fifty-six years."

Seventy-six-year-old widow, Sarah Miller, sat stoically in the center of the first row staring at the coffin. Her ivory hair contrasted with her high collared black dress. Her cane leaned against her knee.

"He was a father who trained his sons to be Godly men and to serve the Lord in their chosen professions."

Micah Miller, the rugged eldest son sitting to the right of his mother, nervously ran his large, calloused hand through his reddish brown hair. His blue eyes brimmed with tears as the depth of his grief consumed him. His father had taught him everything about life from how to farm, to build a barn, to repair tools, to raise a family and to run a business. Now River View Farm on the banks of the Saco River was his responsibility. Micah feared he would never be able to fill his father's shoes.

The Honorable Benjamin Miller sat to the left of his mother. This dignified, slender gentleman with his dark brown hair graying at the temples and wire rimmed glasses was dressed in a suit imported from London. Benjamin was the first man in Fryeburg to wear his hair short and his trousers long, eschewing his pony tails and knee breeches. He was Fryeburg's favorite son, a Harvard graduate, attorney in Philadelphia, the first preceptor of Fryeburg Academy, the first attorney in Oxford County, a former post master and currently Associate Justice of the Court of Common Pleas.[3] His elegant, federal style home and law office sat at the corner of River and Main Streets, a short walk from River View Farm. Filled with concern for his mother, he gently held her frail hand. His parents had been inseparable partners in life. For over five decades they had carved a thriving farm out of the wilderness, raised a family and served their church and community. She had remained constantly by his side during his two years of declining health. How would she fare without his father?

The youngest son, Ethan, was not present. He had left Fryeburg in 1800 to own and operate a successful cabinet making business. He, his wife Olivia and their six children lived in Williamsburg, Virginia.

"James often said, 'The Lord saw fit to take my beloved daughter, Abigail, from us in 1780 but He has blessed me two fold with two daughters-in-law who I could not love more'."

Grace Peabody Miller, seated to the right of her husband Micah, bravely fought back tears. Growing up in Boston before and during the American Revolution, she rarely saw her father who spent much of his time at sea. After her mother died and her father's ship had been destroyed by the British, her grandfather sent her to live with the Millers. In spite of the recent loss of his own daughter, James Miller loved the lonely and frightened child. A charming extrovert who readily spoke her mind, she complemented her reticent and soft spoken husband.

Silver generously streaked the black curly hair of Hannah Chase Miller who sat to the left of her husband, Benjamin. A quiet, reserved Quaker from Philadelphia she had blossomed into a gracious, refined woman, a perfect helpmeet for her dignified husband.

25

"Everyone knows his grandchildren were his pride and joy." There were many chuckles and nods of agreement from the congregation.

Mrs. Elizabeth Miller Endicott, called Libby, arrived from Boston with her two youngest children three weeks ago to help her mother and grandmother. Like her mother Grace, she was a strikingly beautiful woman. Her short sleeved, black silk, empire waist dress caused quite a stir a few moments earlier when she entered the conservative congregation. As the oldest grandchild, she had the most memories of her grandfather. They had spent hours reading Scripture and books. He was the first to ask her what she had learned in school each day. He was bursting with pride when she was hired as an instructress to the first class of young ladies at Fryeburg Academy in June of 1806.

Libby's younger sister, Sarah Alden Miller, called Sadie, lived in a silent world of beauty. Suffering a serious hearing loss as a child, she did not hear the eulogy as she studied the shades of white and purple of the lilacs. Unlike her elegant sister, she wore a simple cotton dress with her long brown braid draping down her back. Uncomfortable in crowds, she preferred the solitude of her art studio where she painted magnificent landscapes. At the age of thirteen, she sold her first painting to her grandfather, who proudly displayed it in the front hall. During his later years, he enjoyed quietly sitting in Sadie's studio watching her paint. Sometimes love does not need words.

Alden James Miller, Micah and Grace's son, had the most gratitude for his grandfather's wisdom and forgiveness. At the age of sixteen, the handsome and cocky lad left the family farm for Harvard College. He never knew how his father learned of his drunken indiscretions in the taverns of Cambridge. Alden had never seen his soft spoken father so outraged as the day he appeared at Harvard to take his son home. His father's angry words such as "disgrace and failure" seared into his memory. It was his grandfather who had intervened on his behalf one solemn evening. He challenged Alden to repent from his past and to move forward with his life and challenged Micah to forgive his son as his Heavenly Father has forgiven him.

Jacob Freeman Miller looked exactly like his mother Hannah with his black, curly hair, gray eyes and long black eye lashes. Benjamin, who had been frustrated with ten year old Jacob's failures in school, could not understand his son's inability to learn to read and write. It was Grandfather who came to his defense and encouraged him to develop his talents in farming and woodworking.

Seated beside him was his blond, green-eyed wife, Katherine Wiley Miller. Their two young sons, Elijah James and Daniel Chase were spending the night at Grandmother Wiley's house in North Fryeburg.

Jacob's sister, Abigail appreciated her grandfather's respect for her mind. He discussed politics and theology with her as if she was his equal and encouraged her to apply for the vacant position of instructress at Fryeburg Academy. He never disapproved of her helping her father in his law practice nor mentioned that at her age she should be married.

"James Miller never thought too highly of himself; he was a humble servant who answered wrath with a quiet word. He treated others equally with respect and dignity."

Sitting in the second row with Widow Abigail Osgood was Limbo, an elderly African slave weeping silently. "The ground is level at the foot of the cross," James explained when he invited Samuel Osgood's slave into his home over fifty years ago. James' acceptance and respect served as a model for his children. Long before teaching at Fryeburg Academy, young Benjamin taught Limbo to read and write. Limbo faithfully sat by James' bedside for an hour every day and was with him when he died.

"James Miller was never too busy to help a neighbor or to listen to a concern."

Mr. Walker silently nodded as he remembered thirty years ago when James and Micah had helped him repair a barn. Mrs. Page remembered when James delivered a wagon filled with firewood to their farm when she was a young girl. Her father had been sick in bed for weeks and winter was approaching. Fifteen years ago the Dressers discovered a large burlap sack filled with potatoes, carrots and squash secretly left on their back door step. Doubtlessly there were many in the congregation silently remembering James Miller with gratitude.

No one noticed the thin, gaunt latecomer standing outdoors on the church steps listening to the eulogy. He placed a large canvas bag filled with his remaining worldly possessions by his feet.

As the congregation sang A Mighty Fortress is our God James Miller's two sons and two grandsons slowly carried the coffin down the aisle, down the stairs and onto Micah's awaiting wagon. Benjamin's carriage behind the wagon was reserved for Sarah, Grace and Hannah to ride. Walking in the shade of giant elm trees the entire congregation followed the family down the short distance from the church to the village cemetery. In the center of the cemetery was one of the earliest gravestones which read:

Abigail Elizabeth Miller
Beloved Daughter of James and Sarah Miller
Born February 2, 1767
Died December 24, 1780

James Miller was laid to rest beside his daughter's grave. Reverend Hurd spoke, "We are gathered here today as the people of God to find comfort in the truth of the Scriptures, 'I am the way, the truth and the life. No one comes to the Father except through Me.'[4] Though James Miller is no longer with us in body we have the assurance that he is present with his Heavenly Father."

Reluctantly, Micah left his father's grave to help his family into his wagon and slowly headed down River Street to the farm. Hannah and Kate climbed into the carriage with Benjamin as Jacob and Alden walked back to the farm. Only Abigail recognized the desolate man leaning against the fence, unmoving as if uncertain as what to do next.

"Mr. Pierce? Mr. Joshua Pierce, is that you?" she asked shyly. Joshua Pierced had served as her father's assistant in the law firm from 1804 – 1810 before he left to begin his own practice in Salem. Although he had lived at the Oxford House, he took his evening meals with the family. "Do you not remember me? I am Abigail Miller."

"Why Abigail, look at you all grown up! You were a mere child when I left. Did you attend Fryeburg Academy as planned?"

"Of course I did. I am now an instructress."

"Of course you are," he smiled gently.

"And I assist Papa with research and preparation for cases."

"I always knew you would do whatever you set your mind to." He looked down uncomfortably. "I am very sorry for your loss."

"We are very sorry for your loss as well. How did you learn the funeral was today?"

"I did not. I was here for a visit. Your grandfather and I had corresponded regularly since..." He looked around nervously.

"How did you get here?"

"I walked."

"Sir, you must be exhausted! Please come immediately to our house and take a rest. It will be quiet while all of us are at the farm," she invited as they left the cemetery.

Abigail unlocked the front door of the stately home and the two of them stepped into the coolness of the large foyer. Mr. Pierce put his canvas bag down on the floor and stared at the four paintings hanging on the left wall. "Did Sadie paint these?" he asked incredulously.

"Yes, Papa commissioned her to paint the view behind the house in each of the four seasons. She calls them 'Portraits of Change'."

The first painting was a summer landscape of the one large maple tree in the meadow. Every imaginable shade of green was used in the leaves, grass and mountainside. A brown rabbit was hiding among the tall grass, a robin was guarding her chicks in a nest high in the branches and a gray squirrel was climbing the trunk. The azure sky was dotted with fair weather clouds.

The second painting was a riot of autumnal color. Shades of red, orange, yellow and brown captured the brilliance of the fall foliage. The rabbit was hiding in a pile of leaves, Canadian geese were flying south in a cloudless, sapphire sky and a squirrel sat contently on the lowest branch holding an acorn in its front paws.

He studied the winter scene. Sunlight glistened on ice cycles and snow. Rabbit tracks crisscrossed the front of the tree before disappearing into a rabbit hole near its base. Two blackcapped chickadees huddled together on a branch. The forth painting captured the dreariness of early spring in fifty shades of grays and browns. Patches of mud peeked through dirty snow. Boot prints led to and from the sap bucket hanging on the spile drilled into the tree. The brown rabbit sat on its haunches peering intently at the colorless sap dripping into the pail.

"May I get something for you to eat, sir?"

"No thank you. May I please have a seat? I feel quite tired."

"Mr. Pierce, please take a rest in the upstairs, back bed-room. The house will be quiet all afternoon. Papa will be delighted to see you again after all these years. How long has it been?"

"Nine years. I left for Salem shortly after Libby left for Boston." Joshua Pierce had been fond of Libby, but alas was too late in articulating his affections. Libby married Edward Endicott, a wealthy Boston merchant and friend of the Peabody family.

"Mr. Pierce, my family will be expecting me at the farm."

"Please go join them. I think I require an hour of rest and solitude." He headed up the front staircase as she walked out the door.

As Micah and the wagon approached the farm he saw the open barn door and heard a gunshot.

II

The Incidents

"Grace, get everyone into the house," Micah commanded as he sprang off the wagon and ran into the barn. He found Mr. Weston, from the farm across the street, pointing an ancient musket at two shabbily dressed strangers.

"Tell that crazy, old man to put down that gun before someone gets hurt!" the first stranger demanded.

"Who are you calling old?" Mr. Weston yelled. "I found these horse thieves trying to steal your horses! That is despicable, I tell you. You wait for the finest man in Fryeburg to die, and when the entire family is at the funeral, you sneak in here to steal their prized horses. Despicable, I say!"

Micah was a humble man but he was proud of his horses which he had bred for decades for their size and strength. "Thank you, Mr. Weston. I will handle it from here," Micah gently took the musket and aimed it between the eyes of the stranger."

"Micah Miller is the best shot in Fryeburg. If I were you, I would not make any sudden moves," Mr. Weston warned.

"Who are you and why are you trespassing on my property?" Micah calmly questioned as Benjamin and his family pulled up in their carriage.

Observing the situation Benjamin whispered to Hannah, "Quickly get Kate inside and lock all the doors. I fear we have been discovered."

Hannah squeezed his hand and calmly led Kate up the front steps.

"I caught these horse thieves red handed!" Mr. Weston explained excitedly to Benjamin. "It is despicable I tell you."

"We ain't no horse thieves! My name is Henry Greene and this here is John Fletcher. We have been employed by Mr. Alexander Hayes from Williamsburg, Virginia to retrieve his rightful property, a slave named George. We've seen him run up from the river into this here barn. Don't want no trouble," he nodded toward the gun. "Just hand over the slave and we will be off with no questions asked."

"Mr. Greene, you have a problem. You have been caught trespassing on private property to steal my brother's horses. I fear I will have to hand you over to the authorities."

"I told you. We ain't horse thieves. We are here to capture a slave."

"That poses another problem," Benjamin continued. "There are no slaves here, but there are two of the finest horses in Fryeburg. I am placing you under arrest."

"You don't dare arrest us. We will tell the judge all about how you all have been smuggling slaves up to Montreal for the past thirteen years."

Benjamin smiled, "Forgive me for not introducing myself. I am the Honorable Benjamin Miller. I am the judge. Do you have any evidence to support your allegations? Do you have any witnesses who will testify in court? I thought not."

"You can arrest us for trespassing but you can't arrest us for stealing horses. Are there any horses missing?" he countered.

"Mr. Greene, your point is well taken. We cannot prove you are horse thieves because the horses are still here. We will drop all charges if you two leave town quietly and never return," Benjamin offered.

"Not without that slave. We ain't returning to Virginia empty handed. Not while that slave is hiding right here in this barn."

Jacob and his cousin Alden arrived on the scene.

"I told you there are no slaves here." Ephraim Weston explained. "I know everything that goes on in these parts. My room is on the second floor," he pointed to the house across the street, "with one window facing the river and the other facing this property. I sit in my window with my spy glass watching the birds, the wildlife. I can see boats going up and down the river. Believe me I would know if there was a slave here."

Micah turned pale. How much did Mr. Weston know?

"He is hiding in the hay!" Mr. Greene accused. The Miller men silently stared at the loose hay strewn on the barn floor. Benjamin swallowed hard. Micah clenched his jaw.

"Are you calling me a liar?" Mr. Weston shouted as he took a pitch fork and stabbed at the hay. He winked at Jacob. "Are you boys going to help me or are you going to let an old man defend your good names?"

Jacob took the pitch fork and gingerly poked in the hay. To his amazement no one was there! "Are you satisfied?" he asked.

Mr. Greene studied Jacob's black curly hair and olive complexion and grew suspicious. "Where are you from, boy?"

"I was born and raised in Fryeburg."

"I have captured quadroons who are whiter than you."

Jacob put down the pitch fork. No one in Fryeburg knew the secret that his mother, Hannah, was born a slave to a mulatto mother and white father on a Virginian plantation. After her father and master died in the Revolutionary War, she was sold to an elderly Quaker couple in Philadelphia who loved her as their granddaughter. It was at the Chase's boarding house where Benjamin met and fell in love with the light-skinned Hannah. He bought her, brought her to Fryeburg, granted her freedom, and married her.

Benjamin had been furious the day he learned that ten-year-old Jacob had discovered the legal documents and the secret about his mother. He had promised his father he would tell no one. He never told his sister, his own wife or mentioned it to his mother.

Jacob knew from reading his Uncle Ethan's letters from Virginia that quadroons were people with one African grandparent and three white grandparents. People like him and his sister with one African great grandparent and seven white great grandparents were labeled octoroons. He also knew from his uncle's letters that white fathers often sold their racially mixed children. For the first time in his life he realized the only thing that protected him from a life of slavery was the honor and virtue of his father.

Benjamin protectively put his hand on Jacob's shoulder. "This is my son. How dare you trespass on my parents' farm, attempt to steal my brother's horses and now insult my family! Micah, give me the gun, and I will shoot him myself."

"Benjamin, you are a terrible shot. You are apt to miss and kill my horse." Nervous laughter broke the tension.

"I don't know how you all do it, but you won't get away with it this time!"

Micah put down the gun. He hoped no one noticed that his hands were trembling. "Get off my property and do not come back."

"All this excitement is not good for my heart!" Mr. Weston declared. "Jacob, be a good lad and help me home."

"Yes, sir." Jacob grabbed the elderly gentleman's arm and slowly crossed the street, heading toward the Weston's front yard.

Once they were safely out of earshot he cleared his throat. "Jacob, please tell your uncle that one of his black lambs have strayed into my barn," he whispered. "Please have him gone by day break."

That evening Benjamin and his family quietly sat around the black walnut, drop leaf dining room table. The table, like the matching black walnut side board and the rest of the furniture, was custom designed and built by Ethan Miller before he left for Virginia in 1800. As the sun was setting Benjamin lit three oil lamps – one on the dining room table and two on the outside wall directly across from the looking glass over the mantel. The mirror reflected the lights of the lamps making the room appear brighter.

The simple act of lighting an oil lamp caused quite a stir six years ago. Benjamin had invited his parents, Micah and his family to dinner one evening and surprised them with his new purchase.

"Mercy! It is like daylight," Sarah gasped.

"It is a blessing. No more reading by the dim, smoky candle light," James admired.

"I must tell you this is revolutionary. I can sew as easily in the evenings as during the day," declared Grace excitedly.

"I could use my evenings to draw if I had adequate light," agreed Sadie.

"Papa, can we buy some for our house?" Alden asked.

Micah eyed the lamp suspiciously. "What kind of fuel does it use? How does it work?"

"It uses whale oil. One of my clients has a brother in New Bedford who sells whale oil."

"I think it would be very exciting to go out to sea and harpoon whales," Alden commented enviously. His maternal grandfather, William Peabody, had owned a ship building and a trading company in Boston before the American Revolution. He spent his childhood listening to Grace's stories about his grandfather's travel and reading books about the sea and ship building. To go whaling would be the adventure of a life time.

"I do not see the point of wasting money on whale oil when we have a ready supply of tallow to make our own candles," Micah countered.

"But, Papa, candles are dirty and smoky. It is a nuisance to constantly trim the wicks. It would take ten of our candles to make the light equal to one of these lamps," Sadie argued.

"The day I harpoon a whale in the Saco River, is the day we will have oil lamps." Micah was a fiercely independent and self-sufficient man. "Benjamin, what will happen when all the whales are gone?"

"The oceans are filled with whales!" Benjamin replied.

Micah shook his head, "Any hunter will tell you if you kill animals faster than they can reproduce, you will eventually wipe out the entire population. Look at beavers. Fur trappers have to go further north and west into the wilderness to trap."

"Whales are not beavers," Benjamin contradicted.

Eventually River View Farm came to depend on oil lamps for illumination. However, Micah always had a good year's supply of candles stored in the tin candle safe for the day whales disappeared from the oceans.

Micah knocked on the back door and quickly let himself in closing the door behind him.

"Welcome. Come in," Benjamin invited.

Micah put his forefinger to his lips and whispered, "Shhhh. I was followed."

Silently Benjamin closed the venetian blinds and drew the drapes.

"Mr. Greene is watching the farm. I left Alden home with the women and children. Please do not argue with me tonight, Benjamin. I am finished. Those men in the barn were armed. Do you know how many hours a day Sadie spends alone painting in her studio? She would never hear anyone approaching."

"I agree. During the past thirteen years we have grown complacent and careless while the village has grown crowded."

"Father, you made a promise," Jacob reminded.

"I do not intend to break my promise; I merely plan to modify it."

"The problem is what to do with the slave in the Weston's barn? The houses are being watched. Who will risk being caught by armed men?"

"I will go," Mr. Pierce volunteered as he silently entered the dining room from the foyer."

"Mr. Pierce! I had forgotten all about you! Papa, after I met Mr. Pierce in the cemetery I invited him to the house to get some sleep."

"Did anyone see you?" Benjamin asked.

"Many people saw me. However no one spoke to me and I doubt anyone recognized me. Like I said I volunteer to go."

"Mr. Pierce, those men have guns. It could be dangerous," Hannah warned.

Joshua Pierce shrugged, "I have nothing left to lose."

"Perhaps you do not. But that slave has his freedom and possibly his life to lose," Jacob interjected. "How will you not be seen or followed when you leave the house?"

"That is simple. I will go through the tunnel."

The Millers sat there in stunned silence. When Benjamin moved from Philadelphia to Fryeburg in 1792 he had promised a group of abolitionists to use his home as a safe house for slaves escaping to Canada. Ethan designed a secret room in the basement and a granite lined tunnel which went under the main street in the village [1] when he built the house back in 1800. This tunnel served as a safe passage as well as a store room for supplies for escaping slaves.

"Surely, you did not think this was a secret. At least half the town of Fryeburg suspects its existence," Joshua informed. "I had always hoped to see it one day myself."

"We will need a diversion," Jacob suggested. "At midnight Alden will enter the barn and release the horses. Uncle Micah, you come out of the house yelling the horse thieves are in your barn. I am sure the commotion will scare them off."

Although Micah did not want to risk the safety of his horses, he could not think of a better alternative.

"When the coast is clear, you can enter the Weston's barn and retrieve the slave."

"Where do we go from there?" Joshua asked.

Kate volunteered, "Take him to my grandfather's house on Fish Street. No, take him in the barn. Remember to follow the old course of the Saco through Fryeburg Harbor, and not the new canal. Hide the canoe in the bushes. It is a short jaunt from the river to my grandfather's. The farm is very isolated. There are no neighbors to spy upon you."

"Mr. Pierce, let me get you something to eat," Abigail offered.

"I must return home, now," Micah said softly. He felt someone watching him from the shadows as he walked back to the farm house. "Good night, gentlemen," he called over his shoulder to the men lurking behind a tree.

Alden lay on his bed fully dressed waiting for the great clock downstairs to strike twelve. Micah had not informed the rest of the family of the plot and retired to bed with Grace at his customary time. At the first strike of the clock, Alden silently crept down the back staircase by the light of the half moon and entered the kitchen. He quietly opened the door to the back addition, walked through it and then the wood shed before finally entering the barn. He did this without taking one step out doors.

The livestock began to stir uneasily. Alden quickly opened the horses' stalls before opening the barn door about two feet. A slap on the feisty stallion's flank was all it took to start a small stampede of horses out the barn door and up the street.

Alden ran back through the woodshed and addition into the kitchen in time to hear his father yelling as he ran out the front door, "The horses! The horses! Those thieves have stolen my horses!"

Grace, still dressed in her night clothes, ran after her husband. "Alden, get your father's gun. We have horse thieves to capture," she yelled angrily.

Libby poked her head out her opened window, "Mama, what is happening?" Her two children began to whimper then wail.

"Libby, stay in the house with your grandmother and lock all the doors," Grace instructed as Alden ran down the front door carrying his father's rifle.

"What is going on?" Mrs. Weston called from across the street.

"The horse thieves have stolen our horses," Alden yelled.

"There they are, by the river!" Ephraim Weston shouted out his second story window. "This is despicable! I tell you despicable! If you two come near my barn I will shoot both of you," he threatened. The two men ran in the direction of Conway, New Hampshire.

Joshua Pierce had watched the whole episode safely behind a tree half way up a hill. He slowly walked to the barn and quietly opened the door. "George?" he whispered. "George, are you here? The coast is clear. I will take you by canoe down river to another hiding place."

A slender, frightened young man in his mid-twenties slowly climbed down the ladder from the hay loft. "I have brought you some supplies," Joshua handed him a wool blanket and a cloth sack filled with clothing, hat, mittens, soap, candles and two loaves of bread. "I will need your help in paddling." George nodded as he took his supplies and silently followed Joshua to the river.

Several lamps were lit at Benjamin's house as the first horse ran by and turned right onto Main Street headed toward Conway. The second horse ran through Kate's herb garden before turning left onto Main Street.

"Benjamin, I need to borrow your horses," Micah yelled out of breath.

"I will saddle them up," Jacob volunteered as he ran to the stable. A neighbor arrived on horseback. "I will round up the stallion," he offered as he headed off. Several nearby homes lit their lamps as neighbors began pouring into the street.

"One horse just galloped through the church yard headed toward East Fryeburg," Dr. Ruel Barrows pointed. "Horse thieves?"

"I would appreciate your assistance," Micah sighed wearily.

Another neighbor arrived on horseback. "Two horses just trotted toward Frye's Hill heading towards Center Fryeburg."

"Alden and I will go after those two," Micah explained. "Can you and Jacob head up toward East Fryeburg? With any luck you might find her in the pasture at Walker's Farm."

By now at least thirty people were milling around Main Street. "What is this town coming to?"

"Those two should be strung up on the nearest tree. Oh, pardon me, Reverend Hurd, I did not see you standing there."

"May I suggest that those of us not in pursuit of the horses return to our homes and pray for their safe return," the good pastor faced his neighbors and congregants. "Remember the Millers in your prayers for they surely have had a most trying day."

It was almost dawn when the last horse was finally returned to its stall.

III

A New Day

Sarah awoke at dawn realizing for the first time in her life she had no reason to get out of bed. Her husband was gone, her children and grandchildren were grown and no one needed her care or companionship.

Her loom and spinning wheel were stored in the corner of the work room years ago as her arthritis progressed. She could no longer carry buckets of water or cast iron pots. With her diminished eye sight she could no longer read. With some difficulty she got out of bed, walked with her cane over to her dresser and took out a pile of letters from her top drawer.

Elizabeth Alden and Abigail Smith were her two childhood friends back in Weymouth. Elizabeth married William Peabody, a wealthy shipbuilder and merchant and had one daughter, Grace. After Elizabeth's unexpected death in 1781, Grace came to live with the Millers and later married Micah.

Abigail had married an attorney named John Adams. Sarah enjoyed rereading Abigail's letters from the past sixty years because they were filled with eye witness accounts of the Boston Massacre, the Boston Tea Party and the events of the Adams family. It was a collection of stories which began with letters from a lonely, young wife and mother with an absent husband as John spent long periods away in the service of his country. It included political insights from the wife of the second President of the United States. These letters were her prized possessions.

She took the top letter from the pile and struggled to the chair by the window. It did not matter that she could not read it in the semi-darkness, for she had this one memorized.

Quincy, Massachusetts
November 1818

My Dearest Mrs. Miller,
It is with my deepest sorrow that I write our beloved Abigail died two weeks ago. I could not have served my country without the love, support and wisdom of my wife and dear friend.

I do beg your forgiveness for taking the liberty of reading a few of your letters. I now realize your faithful correspondence provided her with much needed friendship and encouragement. For that I am truly in your debt.

It is my only consolation that someday soon Abigail and I shall be reunited after this temporary separation.
Your Humble Servant,
John Adams

Gone. They were all gone. Her parents, her closest friends, her daughter, her dearest James were gone. No one needed her today. They were all gone.

"Micah, you should get some rest," Grace suggested to her bleary eyed husband as he finally entered the kitchen after the last horse was safely returned to its stall.

"The cows do not milk themselves!" he snapped.

Grace held her tongue for she understood the strain and sorrow he felt.

He softened. "That is good advice. After I milk the cows and eat some breakfast, I will take a rest. I am already two weeks behind in planting, what are another few hours?" Breakfast was eaten in exhausted silence. No one mentioned the empty chair at the head of the table.

It was mid-morning when Jacob and Kate headed to the Wiley's house to pick up the boys. Mr. Pierce's canvas bag was hidden in the back. Jacob tipped his hat at several neighbors to say hello.

"It was a wonderful service yesterday."

"Tell your grandmother she is in our prayers."

"Did you get all the horses back in the barn? What is this town coming to when a man cannot leave his barn to go to a funeral?"

"Where are the boys?"

"They spent the night at my grandparents. We are on our way to pick them up." Kate explained.

The question which was left unasked this morning was, "Did Mr. Pierce and the runaway make it safely to the Wiley's barn."

"Katie, I should have told you about my family's avocation before we were married. I am sorry for getting your family involved."

"Jacob, I suspected all along. It is a poorly kept secret. Besides, you will find my family very supportive to your avocation."

"I am sorry. A husband should not keep secrets from his wife."

"It was not your secret to keep. It would have been dishonorable to betray the trust of your family."

"Would you object if I took over the family's avocation? My father and uncle have been doing this for a long time."

"I would love to help you," she replied excitedly. We could build a false bottom to the wagon. No one would expect a young mother with two little children to be transporting slaves."

He smiled at his adventurous wife with gratitude as he reached for her hand. "Please forgive me for keeping secrets." He had promised his father that he would tell no one about his mother's past. Now he wondered if Katie would have married him if she had known the truth. "Please forgive me."

By God's grace last night worked out according to plan. Jacob's father-in-law convinced him it was not safe for George to move while the slave catchers were in town. The exhausted, frightened runaway should stay with the Wiley's for a few weeks.

"Mother, I am leaving for school," Abigail called as she gathered her books.

"Have a good day, dear," Hannah smiled. When she was a young slave growing up on a Virginia plantation she never dreamed one day she would be the mistress of her own home and have a daughter grow up to be a teacher. She watched Abigail walk down Main Street toward Fryeburg Academy, one of the first secondary schools to admit girls.

Benjamin stared with dismay at the pile of papers in front of him. He no longer noticed the large ink stain covering one corner of the Chippendale desk. This past week he had been torn between sitting by his father's bedside and sitting at his desk. He had wisely chosen the better option, but now he had much catching up to do. However, he had one more thing to do first.

"Hannah, I am going to pay Limbo a visit. I shall return within the hour." As he approached the Osgood's home he spied Limbo sitting forlornly by the front window.

"How are you doing, my old friend?" Benjamin greeted.

"I am going to miss your father. It was a beautiful service yesterday seeing the whole family there – his children, grandchildren and great grandchildren. He could be proud of the life he led."

Benjamin nodded, feeling there was something left unsaid.

"Back in my village in Africa the entire family would watch over you when you were dying. No one ever died alone. I always thought…"

Benjamin felt foolish that he realized only now what Limbo had lost. "I am sorry, Limbo. Your life would have been much different if those slavers had not captured you when you were a boy. You would have had your own home and your own family."

"I would not die alone or be forgotten. My name, my story would be passed down through the generations."

"I will not forget you, Limbo. I promise I will not forget."

Hannah realized that the house was strangely quiet. There were no grandchildren getting into mischief, or clients clamoring to see her husband. She grabbed a knife from the kitchen and headed out the front door. The fragrance of lilacs greeted her. She smiled remembering the day a wagon load of scrawny plants arrived fifteen years ago. How excited Jacob was to be planting them with his father! "Someday these bushes will be taller than I am," Benjamin had predicted.

She selected a dozen of the largest lilacs, arranged a bouquet in a glass water pitcher and headed for River View Farm.

"I smell lilacs," Sarah said as Hannah entered the back door.

"They are for you," Hannah smiled.

"Mercy! What a large bouquet. Thank you, dear."

"How are you today, Mother?"

"I am tired. I cannot believe James is gone."

"You need to get some rest."

"It is not yet noon," Sarah argued.

"I will put these by your bed and make us a cup of tea. After our visit, I will help you to your bed and you can fall asleep with the scent of lilacs."

Grace gave her sister-in-law a look of gratitude.

It was noon when the family returned with an exhausted Mr. Pierce sitting in the front of the wagon with Jacob and Kate and two exuberant little boys in the back.

"Nana, did you miss your big boy?" five-year-old Eli asked his grandmother as he scooted out of the wagon. Hannah looked with disapproval at his dirty bare feet.

"She picked him up and kissed him. "I missed both of my boys!"

"Did Grandpa miss me too?"

"Perhaps you should go ask him," she suggested as she helped three-year-old Danny out of the wagon and Eli ran to the back door.

"No running in the house," Kate reminded. Her mother-in-law was so much stricter with the children than her own mother.

Eli obediently walked through the kitchen, the dining room, crossed the foyer and knocked on the door of his grandfather's office just as his grandmother taught him to do.

"Come in," Benjamin distractedly replied.

"Grandpa, did you miss your big boy?" he asked as he poked his head into the large, imposing office. This was the one room which he was strictly forbidden from entering alone. He had to knock and wait for his grandfather's invitation. He did not understand what his grandfather did all day in that big room but he did know that Grandpa was a 'portant man with 'portant books and papers.

Benjamin smiled and opened his arms as Eli ran to him. "I missed you very much," he kissed the top of Eli's curly head. Do you understand why you went for your special visit with Grandma Wiley?"

"Yes, sir. Old Grandpa died and everyone went to church to take him to heaven. Danny and I wiggle too much in church." Two years ago, Eli named his great grandparents Old Grandpa and Old Nana so he would not confuse them with his grandparents. It was a title that James and Sarah wore proudly.

Benjamin laughed, "Elijah James, you are a big boy!"

Jacob delivered Mr. Pierce to the front steps of River View Farm and carried in the canvas bag. Sarah was waiting for him in the drawing room and invited him to sit on the gold and white settee.

"Mr. Pierce, you have been in our prayers daily since we heard about your loss," she began kindly.

"Thank you, Mam." Mr. Pierce averted her gaze and he turned to look out the window. "I am very sorry for your loss as well. Mr. Miller will be greatly missed. I appreciated his encouragement and kind words during these past two difficult years. I have kept every one of his letters and reread them often."

"My husband's invitation to live with us and work on the farm still stands."

"You are very kind and I am most grateful. During my tenure as your son's assistant in his law practice I had grown fond of your family."

"I assure you the feeling is mutual. This is not an act of charity, Mr. Pierce, for my son Micah desperately needs the help on the farm. I fear with the added responsibility of caring for Mr. Miller, we find ourselves behind in the planting and general upkeep. You are a most welcomed addition."

"Thank you, Mam. I will endeavor to work my hardest."

"Is there anything I can do for you, Mr. Pierce?"

"Please call me Joshua."

"Welcome to your new home, Joshua."

Sadie helped her mother tidy the kitchen after the noon meal. She was the only member of the family who had a good night's sleep since she did not hear the ruckus of the night before. "Mama, may I go paint? It has been awhile." When James took a turn for the worse, she had set aside her paints and brushes to help with the around the clock care of her grandfather.

Grace smiled warmly, "Please enjoy yourself for a few hours and be back in time to help with the evening meal."

"Thank you!" Sadie headed to her art studio at the far end of the barn.

Mr. Pierce headed to the fields where the men were working when he spied the two slave catchers across the river. Micah was plowing with the aid of two strong horses as Alden and Jacob planted seeds in the newly plowed soil.

"Welcome," Micah greeted. I am glad to see you. We need all the help we can get."

"Those two men are watching," Mr. Pierce warned.

"We know. Benjamin says if they are not trespassing there is nothing we can do but ignore them."

Sadie packed her basket with clean paint brushes, a palette, and paints, locked her studio door and headed towards Main Street. Although her family did not notice her departure the two strangers from Virginia did. She waved to Aunt Hannah and Kate who were in their yard with Eli and Danny and turned left onto Main Street. After a twenty minute walk she turned down the lane to the Swan's farmhouse. Caleb Swan had been her grandfather's closest friend and his family allowed her to store her easel, stool and a half-finished painting of Swan's Falls in their shed. She quietly set up her easel and art supplies in a shady spot by the waterfall where she could feel the spray of mist. She did not hear the twig snap under the Mr. Greene's foot.

She critically stared at the painting. It was all wrong! There was no sense of movement in the water. She was tempted to throw the canvas in the river and go home. What would her grandfather say? He would have told her not to give up and to learn from her mistakes.

"It looks like she is waiting for someone," Mr. Greene whispered.

"No it don't. It looks like she is painting," Mr. Fletcher contradicted.

After a three hour wait, Mr. Greene shouted impatiently, "Looks like whoever you are waiting for ain't showing up."

Unaware of the danger, Sadie was busy mixing blues and grays, looking up from her pallet to study the light reflecting off the water.

Grace entered the barn asking, "Alden, have you seen your sister? She is not in the house and her studio is locked."

"I will check to see if she is visiting with my mother," Jacob offered as he headed up the street. He found Kate watering the herb garden while Eli and Danny played in the mud. He picked up his muddy, barefoot sons and laughed, "I know a future farmer when I see one. Is Sadie here?"

"Why no. We saw her walk by about three hours ago carrying her art basket."

Micah looked upset when Jacob returned without Sadie. "Has anyone seen those two men? I fear Sadie left to paint at Swan's Falls and they have followed her." He saddled up a horse, grabbed his rifle and galloped off. Jacob quickly saddled a second horse and followed.

Micah would never admit it, but Sadie was his favorite. Libby, fiercely independent, assertive and opinionated was a "Peabody through and through". Micah always knew that Libby would someday leave the farm for the exciting city life in Boston. Alden was a disappointment. Since his indiscretions in Cambridge disgraced the family, Alden displayed very little enthusiasm for farming. But quiet, sweet and talented Sadie needed her father.

"I said it looks like whoever you are waiting for ain't showing up," Mr. Greene repeated as Sadie continued studying the water. "Did you hear me?" he shouted. In exasperation he marched over, grabbed her shoulder and yelled, "I asked you a question."

First startled, then frightened by his sudden appearance, she screamed, grabbed her stool and swung it at his face, breaking his nose. He yelped in pain as Mr. Fletcher lunged forward to grab the stool away from her. Sadie stepped back tripping over the easel with paints and canvas crashing to the ground. Enraged, she kicked him in the shins and bit his right hand as he tried to grab her.

Micah pulled up his horse six yards away and pulled out his rifle. He had a clean shot of the man's back of the head and put his finger on the trigger. Jacob arrived, flung out his arm and knocked the gun barrel skyward as the gun went off.

"I warned you to stay away from my family!"

The men raised their arms in surrender. "We don't want no trouble."

"Trouble is exactly what you got."

"Micah, I must tell you it is almost midnight," Grace scolded as she found her husband sitting in the drawing room in the moonlight staring at his father's empty chair. "You need your rest."

"I cannot sleep."

"Micah, I am so sorry," she affectionately took his large hands into hers. "We will all miss him."

"Yesterday in the barn was the first time I felt fear since…"

"Since you were seventeen years old and you and Mr. Bradley went to hunt the catamount that was killing livestock. You are a very brave man, Micah. We were all afraid yesterday."

"I cannot protect you. I would never forgive myself if anything should happen to this family. That is why you, Sadie and Mother must leave for Boston with Libby.

"Those men will not intimidate me. You shall not send us away."

"Please, Grace…"

"Running away will simply prove that we have something to hide. Besides, there is too much for me to do at this time of year. I will not go!"

Micah put his head in his hands. "Grace, I almost killed a man today. I would have too if Jacob did not stop me. I need you to take Mother and Sadie to Boston with Libby. I need to know my family is safe. Please do it for me."

"I do not know how I could handle traveling with two young children, your elderly mother and Sadie. You know the ship will be crowded and Sadie dreads crowds and strangers."

"I will have Alden accompany you. You shall leave in two days."

IV

Graceless

"Hannah, thank you for having us for supper while Grace and the family are away," Micah greeted as he and Mr. Pierce entered the kitchen.

"Of course, you are family. Mr. Pierce, you are like family to us. We have truly missed you these past nine years."

"I have missed all of you as well. I remember what a fine cook you were, Mrs. Miller."

Hannah, who was a modest woman, blushed. "Cooking is easy. Rounding up everyone for meals is not. Micah, please try to drag your brother out of his office. Abigail, please run upstairs and tell Kate we are ready to eat."

Fifteen minutes later seven adults and two clean, little boys were seated around the dining room table. Benjamin seated at the head of the table said grace. "Our Heavenly Father, the Creator of all good gifts, we thank Thee for the food before us, for the farmer who provided it, and for this home. Please watch over our family who is not with us tonight. Please keep them safe in Your presence. In Jesus precious name we pray. Amen." Micah never realized how much Benjamin sounded like their father.

"Jacob tells me you are all caught up with the planting," Benjamin, who despised farming as a child, made an effort to show interest in his brother's livelihood.

"I could not have done it without the help of Jacob and Joshua. We worked from sunrise to sunset."

Kate did her best to keep Eli still in his seat while she quietly dished out another small helping to Danny.

"Has Fryeburg been affected by the Panic? There is massive unemployment in Boston and Philadelphia."[1] Joshua asked.

"When you are a poor farmer, you tend not to notice."

"Micah, you are too humble," Hannah admonished. "You are a successful business man and a prosperous farmer."

"I only meant that a lack of rainfall or an early frost is a bigger threat to making a living than what happens to bankers and businessmen in the cities. Farmers can live without cities but cities cannot live without farmers. I blame the Second Bank of the United States for this mess."

"The situation is a little more complicated than that," Benjamin explained. "The federal government chartered the Second Bank three years ago to help manage the federal debt incurred by the War of 1812.[2] A war, by the way, President Madison should never have gotten this country involved."

"What choice did he have?" Micah replied.

"Papa, how many times have Mama and Aunt Grace forbade you two to argue about the war?" Abigail implored.

Mr. Pierce laughed. "I have fond memories of your political arguments."

"They are political discussions and not arguments. This is America. My brother has every right to be wrong," Benjamin joked good-naturedly. Micah shook his head. "As I was saying the Second Bank was to manage the federal debt and curb inflation brought on by unregulated state banks."[3]

"Do you mean that the government formed a national bank to fix the state banks? It seems to me if a small bank can create problems, then a large bank will create larger problems." Jacob was not well-read but he was respected for his common sense.

"Most banks are privately own and operate for commercial purposes," Abigail continued. They issued their own version of paper money."

"I thought only the government can mint our money," Hannah interrupted. She remembered listening to Benjamin's lesson plans for Fryeburg Academy back in 1792 when Alexander Hamilton, George Washington's Secretary of the Treasury, devised a monetary dollar system based on the decimal system.[4]

"They issued paper imprinted with a promise to pay in gold or silver on demand. It is not the same as money," Abigail explained.

"I would never hand over my gold and silver to some strangers in exchange for paper," Micah stated.

"There was wild land speculation out west fueled by the credit offered by these state banks. At the same time they were offering credit to finance businesses to create economic growth after the War of 1812. Remember when Libby was complaining how the Endicotts were almost forced out of business during that war and how business has picked up again? Now picture hundreds of businesses becoming prosperous at the same time borrowing money to expand."

"If things were going so well, what went wrong?" Jacob asked.

"Unfortunately, two events happened simultaneously. The first was the banks lent out more than they had gold and silver to back it up. When several large creditors demanded cash payments at the same time, it led to bank failures and panic.

During the Napoleonic Wars European farms and manufacturing were damaged or destroyed. Therefore many Europeans needed to import American goods. As Europe has recovered from the wars, the demand for American farm and manufactured products drastically declined."[5]

"No one should print more paper "money" than they have the actual gold and silver to back it up. That is just plain common sense. That should not be legal," Jacob complained.

"Banks are greedy. They do not work for their money. Instead they try to make a profit from other people's hard earned money," Micah grumbled. "A fool and his money are soon parted,"[6]

"Unfortunately many innocent people are suffering financial hardship. We have much for which to be thankful," Abigail quietly interjected.

"Abigail, you are an insightful young lady," Mr. Pierce complimented. "Your students are indeed fortunate to have you as a teacher."

Jacob trusted the Lord would forgive him for not keeping the Sabbath. After church services, Jacob took Kate and the boys in the wagon to her grandmother's house. As this was their custom during fair weather, no one would grow suspicious. After Sunday dinner, Kate, her mother, grandmother and several sisters-in-law sat in the shade of the large elm tree watching the dozen cousins running barefoot and playing in the yard.

Jacob was indoors with some of Kate's brothers drawing plans when the escaped slave entered the back room. "You must be George," he nodded to the young man.

"Yes, sir."

"My name is Jacob. Pleased to make your acquaintance," he extended his hand.

George timidly shook the hand of a white man for only the second time in his life. "I know some carpentry. I thought I could help. Back in Virginia, a big, red haired carpenter taught me some carpentry and even gave me some old tools."

"I have been thinking about this room for days." He moved the kitchen table and chairs and braided rug. "We can cut a trap door right here and build a hidden room underneath. I think thirteen feet by fourteen feet would be an adequate space. Once we replace the rug and furniture, no one would ever guess it was there. George, we will take you up on your offer.

Do you have family that you want to join you in Canada?"

"I don't know where my brothers are. I hope my little sister and mother could join me someday."

"What about your father?" Jacob innocently asked.

"My father was the one who sold me to his friend. That is where I made my escape. I figured as long as I didn't escape from him directly, my mother and sister would be safe. After all, my master got his money for me, why would he care if I ran off from someone else's plantation.

One day my old friend the carpenter delivered a fancy desk to my new master. On his way back to the wagon he whispers to me, 'if you want to escape meet me at the old oak tree by the pond half a mile from here at nightfall.' I was so scared, I mean suppose this was a trick? Suppose he was a friend of my new master? But there he was waiting for me with a wagon filled with furniture. He put me in one of those wooden crates packed with straw that he packed furniture in. All night long, he made stops to pick up new "furniture". By the time we arrived at somebody's barn the wagon was loaded half with real furniture and half with folks on their way to freedom. They unloaded the crates. The carpenter put those crates back in his wagon and was off to make more deliveries. I feel right sorry that I never thanked him."

Jacob felt ill when he realized that George's father was his master and he sold his own son! He took a good look at the young man. Although George was not as black as Limbo, a pure African, he had distinctively Negroid facial features. He could never pass for white. "We will do our best to rescue your mother and sister. Now we will quickly take some measurements, make a list of supplies before I join the others outside."

Abigail was running late Monday morning as she hurried up Main Street with an armload of books when the Academy's bell struck eight. This bell, the first to toll in the Pequawket Valley, was the pride of Fryeburg. Not only did it summon students to class during the week it also served on Sundays to call the parishioners to services at the Congregational Church.[7]

A classroom of whispering young ladies anxiously watched through the second story window. Miss Miller was never late for anything in her entire life.

"Perhaps she is helping a runaway slave," one student suggested.

"It is a sin to gossip," another remonstrated. "No one knows if those stories are true."

"My father says Judge Miller would never break the law."

"Maybe she stayed up too late with her beau," someone giggled.

"She does not have a beau."

"I think she is a hopeless spinster."

"Maybe she should dress more fashionably. If her father can afford expensive suits for himself he can afford better looking dresses for her."

"Her mother is a Quaker. I do not think they wear fancy frocks."

"It will take more than fancy dresses to find her a husband."

"That is a terrible thing to say."

"Well, she cannot cook, or sew or keep house."

"Perhaps she is wedded to her books. I admire her independence and scholarship."

"Ladies, I do apologize for my tardiness," Abigail rushed to her desk slightly out of breath. "I was up half the night reading and I overslept. We live in exciting times as America is growing as a new nation. It is a time to develop cultural independence from England with a distinctive American language.[8]

"Miss Miller. We speak English. We do not speak American."

"Perhaps it would be more accurate to say we speak an Americanized version of English. Noah Webster is compiling *An American Dictionary of the American Language*. Some of you may remember Mr. Webster for his *Blue Back Speller* that we all used as children."

"Miss Miller, why do we need a new dictionary?"

"We have many new words in our vocabulary which you will not find in a British dictionary." She picked up a piece of chalk and wrote on the blackboard skunk, caribou, chipmunk, muskrat, raccoon and woodchuck. "What do these words have in common?"

"They are animals."

"To be more accurate they are animals native to America. The colonists did not have words for these unfamiliar mammals. They adopted Indian words for them." She wrote more words on the black board: chowder, squash, squaw, succotash, tomahawk and canoe. "These are names of food or items originated with the Indians.

We are also developing our own American literature. Washington Irving has just written *The Sketch Book,* a collection of essays and stories. He is one of the first American authors to win international fame.[9] Many of his stories were written in England about England. However, we will be reading *Rip Van Winkle*, a fanciful, short story which takes place in his home state of New York. Since I have the only copy in town, we will take turns reading aloud. Miss Bradley, you may begin."

Kate settled her two sons in the back of the wagon and then climbed in beside Hannah.

"It is a lovely morning for a ride," Hannah said pleasantly.

They paused on Main Street to say hello to Reverend and Mrs. Hurd. "Good morning, ladies and where are you headed?" he greeted warmly.

That was when Hannah glimpsed Mr. Greene sitting on his horse watching them. "We are bringing some bread and cheese and a bouquet of lilacs to Mrs. Sanborn," she answered as she held up the bouquet. "No one has seen the Sanborns since their child died last month."

"Please tell them they are in my prayers and I will visit tomorrow," he lifted his hat as they passed.

Although Kate tried to keep a distance between the wagon and Mr. Greene, he caught up with them at the top of Walker's Hill.

"Good morning, ladies," he grinned. "I trust your brother-in-law is in possession of all his horses? I ain't no horse thief."

"No sir. You are something far worse," Hannah stated curtly.

"Now, Mrs. Miller, what is a nice Quaker lady like you doing with that rifle. I thought you people were pacifists."

"Yes, Sir, we are," she smiled. "However that is not my gun."

"And I am not a Quaker!" Kate laughed.

"What do you need a gun for?" he asked suspiciously.

"There's a rabid fox in these parts," she lied. "I would be careful being out here by yourself, if I were you."

"That's a pretty big gun for a little lady," he sneered.

Kate aimed the rifle at a nearby maple tree and pulled the trigger. A dead squirrel fell to the ground. "My daddy used to take me hunting with my brothers."

"Katherine, was that really necessary!" Hannah exclaimed as the boys laughed and clapped.

"Good day, Mr. Greene. Keep your eyes out for that fox," Kate smirked and headed down the hill. Mr. Greene remained at the top of the hill watching the wagon head toward East Fryeburg as he scanned the woods for rabid wildlife.

The Sanborn's farm was located in an isolated area not far from the old course of the Saco River and Kezar Pond. Mr. Sanborn warmly greeted the visitors and welcomed them in the house. Mr. Greene watched them through a stand of birch trees. He had no idea what they discussed for those two hours, for he dared not approach any closer. He never suspected that Mr. and Mrs. Sanborn had agreed to build a secret room in their farmhouse.

Abigail returned home late from school and found Uncle Micah, Joshua, Jacob and her father conversing in the dining room. "Did you have a good day at school?" Mr. Pierce asked pleasantly.

"Abigail, could you please help Kate set the table?" Hannah requested as she placed a platter of baked chicken on the table.

"Aunt Abby!" Eli ran to his aunt who picked him up and kissed him on the cheek.

"Were you a good boy today and not make Danny cry?"

"Mostly," he replied evasively.

She carried two large bowls of peas and parsnips to the dining room as Kate brought a basket of bread slices and a small crock of butter to the table.[10]

"I thought you may be interested in this." She handed her father a copy of a broadside.

INDEPENDENCE!!
July 26th, 1819

CITIZENS OF MAINE,

Shall Maine be a free, sovereign and independent State, or shall you and your children remain forever the servants of a foreign Power? This is the true question that is to be settled by your votes on Monday next. The friends of liberty cannot hesitate in the choice between freedom and servitude.

What shall we lose by separation? The privilege of being governed by Massachusetts. What shall we gain? The right of governing ourselves.

The last year we paid Massachusetts EIGHTY EIGHT THOUSAND DOLLARS for governing us. This is proved by the official certificate signed by the Secretary of State. It will cost us less, probably not more than one half of this sum to govern ourselves. Almost the whole of this is now carried to Boston and expended there. Choose freedom and independence and one half of this sum will be saved to the people and the other half will be spent at home.

Six million acres of Lands in Maine are now owned by non-resident land holders; full one third which is owned in England. These lands now pay but a nominal tax. Two thirds of the tax is taken off; and who pays it? It is paid by the Farmers and Mechanics in addition to his own property share of taxes. It is these non-resident land holders who are afraid of taxes. Their land is taxed at two percent, yours at six percent.

They now pay a Boston lawyer one or two thousand dollars a year to manage this business with the legislature. What is taken from their tax is added to yours. Their taxes may be increased but yours will be diminished.

These land holders are now traversing Maine in every direction. They have their agents in pay every quarter, and they are all opposed to your independence.

If you do not wish that you and your children should forever pay the taxes of these nabobs of Massachusetts and England, turn out on the next Monday and give your voices for separation.

FELLOW CITIZENS

The eyes of all America are upon you. Your enemies are active and vigilant, and already boast of their fancied success. We exhort you to turn out in your whole strength. Let not a vote be lost. Leave your private business for a day or half a day or an hour, and convince the world by an overwhelming majority that you deserve

FREEDOM AND INDEPENDENCE.

July 21.[11]

After Benjamin said grace and the food was passed Joshua asked, "What does the Miller family think of Maine becoming the 23rd state?"

"It is about time," Micah declared.

"I do not know why the Province of Maine ever became a part of Massachusetts in the first place," Jacob stated in frustration. "Maine does not even border Massachusetts."

"Back in the 1650's Maine was its own entity. The more powerful Massachusetts Bay Colony purchased the region as propriety in 1677 and retained jurisdiction over it under a new province charter in 1691.[12] Remember back in the 1600's and early 1700's most of the towns were along the coastline, roads were poor or nonexistent and ships sailing up and down the coast were the mode of transportation. Portland or Camden is not that far from Salem or Boston by boat," Joshua explained.

"There were many hard feelings between Maine and the Massachusetts colonial government during the Revolution because they left our coast defenseless. The British attacked towns like Falmouth and Castine ravaging the land, destroying vessels, burning down houses and barns, slaughtering livestock and even kidnapping some of the local leaders,"[13] Benjamin continued.

"I remember when General Washington called up Joseph Frye and his men and stationed them in Falmouth,"[14] Micah said.

"That was after the British burned Falmouth. That is like closing the barn door after the horses escape," Benjamin complained.

Micah groaned, "Could you please select another expression?"

"To add insult to injury, Massachusetts then demanded endless taxes, troops and provisions."

"That is why I and forty-two others form Fryeburg under Captain Philip Eastman went to Fort Burroughs in Portland in the summer of 1814 to protect it from the British," Jacob explained.[15] "Nearby Nova Scotia is filled with British and could have easily invaded us by ship. We could not depend upon the support from Boston."

"Massachusetts did not want to enter the war in the first place. Libby said that the war crippled the manufacturing and commerce in Boston. It was financially devastating," Abigail continued.

"The Revolution was financially devastating to the colonies too and that did not stop Massachusetts from wanting to fight that war. Sometimes wars must be fought to protect our freedom," Micah contradicted.

"Not everyone in Boston agreed with the Patriots. Do you remember Mother's letters from Mrs. Adams and Mrs. Peabody describing how thousands of Loyalists in the city were forced to return to England or to relocate to Nova Scotia?[16] Many Loyalists throughout the colonies lost their homes and businesses and even their lives. Not every American wants to fight in wars," Benjamin argued.

"Are you two going to bicker about the Revolutionary War as well?" Hannah raised one eyebrow."

"Forgive me, Hannah. You did not graciously invite me to your home, so you can listen to us argue," Micah apologized.

"Mr. Pierce, did you know that Benjamin will help write the Maine state constitution this October?" she attempted to change the subject.

"Let us not be premature. We must wait until after the vote to see if Maine will become a state," Benjamin reminded. "Not everyone in the province wants this."

"The Federalists are against it," Micah explained.

"That statement is an over simplification. The Federalist Party of George Washington, John Adams and Alexander Hamilton has been unraveling since the War of 1812. Even John Quincy Adams, was once a Federalist but now he is serving in President Monroe's Cabinet.[17]

I think in terms of the 'old Maine' and 'new Maine'. The older towns and cities established along the coast were founded before the Revolution and even as far back as the seventeenth century. It is true that the populations of these towns tend to be Federalist and Congregational.[18]

Many of the newcomers who settled in Maine after the Revolution settled further inland and were Baptists and Methodists as well as Congregationalists. They also tended to be members of the Democratic-Republican Party. The population in Maine at the onset of the War in 1777 was 42,000 and now it is almost 300,000.[19] That is an increase of seven fold in forty-three years. These people, like the founding fathers of Fryeburg, are independent pioneers ready to begin new farms, industries and towns.

The older, established coastal towns have long held ties and deep roots with Massachusetts. They share the same religious, political, social and economic history. They are presently benefitting financially from a close relationship with Massachusetts. In addition, there are wealthy and influential people in Massachusetts benefitting from owning large land holdings. These two groups do not wish to sacrifice their economic success to thousands of new comers.[20] I do not believe it is as much as denomination or political party as to finances."

Jacob critically studied his family. Red headed Uncle Micah "was a Miller" who resembled Old Grandpa. His dark haired father "was a Bradford", resembling his grandmother Sarah and the numerous members of the Bradford clan. He remembered when his mother's hair was once as black as his. Her hair did not appear to be as curly as his, when she pulled it back and up into a bun. Her skin was only a shade or two darker than his father's. Unlike George, she clearly had Caucasian facial features. He guessed she might be a quadroon or perhaps an octoroon. Old Nana had always declared that Abigail "was a Bradford", for she had straight, dark hair like her father. No one would ever suspect there was a drop of African blood in her veins.

He smiled at his green-eyed, freckled faced, blond wife. Elijah had a mop of unruly, dark brown curls and a glint of mischief in his warm brown eyes. Daniel had his mother's green eyes and the Bradford straight, dark hair.

"Why did Mr. Greene mistake me for a quadroon?" Jacob wondered.

"I received two letters from Grace today," Micah changed the subject.

"It is a wonderful thing to receive mail once a week, instead of once every two weeks,"[21] Hannah said.

"They arrived in Boston safely but Mother found the journey to be most vexing. Apparently there were several men cursing and cussing and spitting tobacco on the ship. But she is now enjoying herself at Libby's and spending time with the great grandchildren. Grace cannot believe how much Boston has changed since she was a girl."

"Who is running the creamery while Grace is away?" Kate asked. Grace had a successful business selling butter, cheese and milk to the Oxford House, a few merchants and several other families in the village who did not farm. Although Micah provided for all the family and farm needs, it was Grace's business which brought in the much needed extra cash. "I would be willing to take over in her absence. I helped my grandmother make cheese and butter when I was a girl. If I could take the boys to the farm with me, I could help," Kate volunteered.

Kate, who grew up with the freedom and hard work on a rural farm, found village life to be stifling. Her herb and flower gardens were not enough to fill her days. She was not content to occupy her time in lady-like endeavors such as reading, embroidering and sewing like her mother-in-law.

Micah looked relieved. "That would be most helpful, if it would not be too much of a burden."

Kate and two excited, barefoot, little boys entered the barn shortly after breakfast. "Papa, I am going to feed the chickens and collect eggs," Eli boasted. "Danny is helping Mama, because he is a baby."

"I am not a baby!" Danny whined.

"Of course you are not a baby," Jacob consoled. "Babies cannot help their mothers."

"Someday we will own our own farm and Eli will have plenty of chores to keep him busy," Kate stated wistfully.

"Someday," Jacob promised. "I have set out the milk pans."

"It does not feel natural having Grace and the children gone," Micah lamented as attached the mare to the plow. "Joshua, I am sorry. I should have thought before I spoke," he apologized.

"What kind of horses are these?" Joshua changed the subject.

"They are work horses. Uncle Micah has been breeding horses for their strength and stamina for years."

"I despise oxen. They are slow and stupid. These horses are intelligent and gentle. They are not fast but a farmer needs a strong horse, not a fast one."

"What is her name?" Joshua asked as he stroked the animal's soft muzzle.

"I believe Donatello likes you," Jacob commented as he attached her mate to the plow. "This is Michelangelo, Mike for short."

"Donatello and Mike are strange names for horses."

Micah laughed. "That is Leonardo da Vinci, and Giotto. Sadie named the horses after famous painters."

"I hate to tell you but Donatello and Giotto are mares."

"That is why we call them Donna and Gia. I confess that I cannot say no to my Sadie."

Eli and Danny loved working on the farm and accompanying their mother in Uncle Micah's wagon with the big horses, as Kate delivered milk, eggs and butter through the village.

"I hope Nana does not miss us too much," Eli sighed with concern.

Micah sat down for supper exhausted but contented. Despite a late start planting and Alden's absence his crops would carry them through the winter. No one had seen or heard from Mr. Greene and his crony for over a month. "I received a letter from Grace this morning," his face was beaming. "The Bradfords had a family reunion at the homestead back in Weymouth. Mother spent the week meeting fifty nieces and nephews. Sadie spent the week painting a picture of the homestead and will give it to Mother as a gift. Best of all, after six weeks away, the family will be back next week."

It was late afternoon when the wagon pulled up in front of River View Farm. Alden was helping his grandmother down when Micah ran from the barn. "Welcome home!" he bellowed as he helped Grace from the wagon and embraced her in a bear hug. "How was Boston?"

"It was crowded, dirty and noisy! I am delighted to be home."

"Mother, did you enjoy your visit?"

"It was wonderful to see my brother Jacob and the family after all these years. I fear the journey has worn me out," she clung tightly onto her grandson's arm. "I would never have managed if it was not for Alden. I know it was a sacrifice to let him go with us, but it was a blessing to have him with me."

Alden smiled at his grandmother. "Let me help you to your room. You will feel better after a nap," he said gently.

For the first time Micah noticed Sadie's absence. "Where is Sadie?"

"Micah, we need to talk."

"I will unload the trunks and bring them into the house," Joshua offered.

"Has something happened to Sadie?" Micah asked swallowing his panic.

"I must tell you our daughter has never been better. She has decided to stay in Boston."

"For how long? Why?"

"She is planning to stay indefinitely."

"And you allowed this without consulting me?"

"It is not our decision to make. Sadie is thirty-one years old and capable of making her own decisions. You allowed Libby to live in Boston when she was only twenty. I did not feel the need to consult you in this matter.

Libby is the only friend Sadie ever had. You know when Libby left, Sadie was lost. All she did was paint. She communicated with very few people outside of the family.

But in Boston, she became alive! You should have seen her expression the first time she saw Boston Harbor. She bought yards of canvas and made every shade of blue imaginable and began to paint with renewed excitement. Libby's children adore her and she has begun giving drawing lessons. Libby gave a few parties in her honor. Some very distinguished families have commissioned her for paintings and murals. She is meeting other artists. Micah, if only you could see how happy she is!"

He felt the joy of having his family home slowly evaporate. Sadie, his Sadie, was not returning home.

V

The Suitor and the Scholars

Although it was Thursday afternoon, Ebenezer Frye Walker was scrubbed clean and dressed in his Sunday best as he rode his horse to the imposing home of the Honorable Benjamin Miller. Why did he ever let his mother talk him into this? Mrs. Walker and Hannah Miller would often converse amiably after church services each week. Eben thought Mrs. Miller to be a kind, humble and thoughtful woman. On the other hand, Eben was intimidated by Mr. Miller's formidable intelligence and knowledge. How would he ever carry on a conversation with the judge? Of course Eben knew Jacob since elementary school. But he was invited this evening to "get better acquainted with Abigail." Why did he let his mother talk him into this?

Hannah was convinced that Eben Walker was the last decent bachelor in Fryeburg. He kept the Sabbath, did not smoke or chew tobacco, did not frequent the local taverns or take the Lord's name in vain. Both she and Mrs. Walker were concerned about finding suitable mates for their youngest children and decided they would discreetly create opportunities for their children to become acquainted.

To Eben's relief Jacob was in the door yard to greet him as he dismounted from his horse. "You should come to supper more often. My mother has been cooking all day!" Jacob greeted.

Bare footed Elijah came running to his father in tears. "Nana says I must put on my shoes like a gentleman. I told her I do not want to be a gentleman. I want to be a farmer!"

Eben stifled a laugh. Perhaps the evening may not be terrible after all. Jacob picked up his son. "Nana made me wear my shoes when I was a boy. You can wear your shoes at the table and then take them off later." That compromise appeased him as he trotted back to the house.

Eben, a simple but hard working farm boy, surveyed the formal dining room. He heard his mother discussing the Miller's white china imported from London and imprinted with blue scenery of the English country side.[1] This was quite the contrast to the Walker's stoneware. Of course the Walkers did not have a separate room just to eat in; they ate on a simple pine table in front of the cooking hearth. He and his siblings were not required to wear their shoes during the summer. He guessed he was not a gentleman, but a farmer.

"Mr. Walker, how kind of you to join us," Benjamin greeted.

"It was kind of you to invite me, sir," he nervously replied as he took his seat at the table next to Jacob but across from Abigail.

"Mr. Walker, have you met Mr. Pierce?" she motioned to the man seated to her left who appeared to be fifteen years older than Abigail. "Mr. Pierce worked as an attorney for my father years ago."

"Oh. I thought you were a farmer who worked for Micah Miller," Eben replied.

"I am a man of many talents," Joshua Pierce joked.

"Mr. Pierce was like a member of the family," Hannah explained. "When he returned to town we insisted that he join us for evening meals, like the old days."

"I am pleased to make your acquaintance, sir," Eben nodded. His mother would be pleased with his good manners.

He glanced at the meal spread before him. There was baked chicken with biscuits and gravy, peas, carrots, spinach and tomato slices.

"Mr. Walker, what do you think of Maine becoming our 23rd state?" Abigail asked.

Although he had not paid much attention to the talk about Maine's future statehood, he realized that some people felt strongly about each side of the issue. "Well, I guess it does not matter much to the corn if it is growing in Maine or Massachusetts," he stated diplomatically.

Abigail laughed. "You sound like my brother. Father is going to Portland next month to help write the state's constitution."

"Sir, my father always says you are the smartest man in Fryeburg. If anyone from Fryeburg should write the constitution, it should be you." Eben sincerely complimented his host.

"However we must remember that Alabama, a slave state, has just been admitted to the Union. I understand that Missouri is applying for statehood as well. They would be the first territory from the Louisiana Purchase to become a state. I hear they want to be a slave state. Can you imagine what will happen if the entire Louisiana Purchase west of the Mississippi become slave states. Maine statehood will be a small consolation if we become a nation of slaves!" Hannah interjected.

Eben looked at her in astounded silence. His mother never spoke of politics nor contradicted his father in front of the family."

"Hannah Dear, you speak the truth," Benjamin respectfully concurred.

"Mr. Walker, now do you understand why I dine here every evening. The wonderful meals are second only to the stimulating conversations," Mr. Pierce smiled. "I agree, Mrs.

Miller. I fear this country is rapidly becoming two nations – a free nation and a slave nation."

"I believe this could lead to violence and ultimately to a civil war," Benjamin shook his head.

"Father, do you really think so?" Jacob asked.

"Yes, I do. Perhaps not within my lifetime, but within your lifetime or their lifetime," Benjamin nodded to the two little boys who were trying their best not to wiggle at the table.

"Perhaps we will end slavery peacefully like England did," Abigail suggested hopefully.

Eben did not realize that England had slaves nor did he realize the English ended it.

"England does not need African slaves, for they have the Irish," Mr. Pierce stated in derision. Joshua's maternal grandparents who emigrated from Ireland relayed many tales of British cruelty.

"Mr. Pierce, we cannot solve all the world's problems at one meal," Benjamin admonished. "Tonight we discuss the statehoods of Maine and Missouri. Perhaps tomorrow night we will solve the plight of the Irish."

Eben wondered if every meal of the Millers' included political discourse.

"Mr. Walker, do you know of William Wilberforce?"

"Is he from Brownfield?"

She laughed, "No he is the member of the British Parliament who convinced England to ban slavery."[2]

"It is a small victory. Most of their slaves do not live in England. They are condemned to work the sugar cane plantations in the West Indies like Barbados and Jamaica. The British are growing wealthy by selling and exporting African slaves to the sugar plantations and importing sugar without one slave stepping foot in England. They need to ban slavery in their territories as well," Hannah continued.[3]

Eben did not know where sugar came from. He only knew it was expensive and his family could not afford it. That is why they made their own maple sugar every spring. He spied the familiar maple sugar stored in the Miller's porcelain sugar bowl. Surely, Judge Miller could afford white sugar! Then he surmised that Mrs. Miller refused to buy sugar from the West Indies. He felt Abigail looking at him as he was thinking of something clever to say. "This is the best bread pudding I ever had. Did you make this?"

"Heavens no! I do not cook." Abigail waved her hand dismissively.

"Oh," he responded awkwardly.

"Katie made it," Jacob patted his wife's hand and smiled.

"Papa, do I have to sit here all night?" Eli complained.

"Elijah, you and your brother have behaved like perfect gentlemen," Hannah complimented her grandsons. "You may be excused."

Eli sprinted out the door with Danny close behind. Eben wished he could have followed them as he stifled a yawn.

"Are we boring you, Mr. Walker?" Abigail teased.

"Abigail, we farmers get up before dawn," Jacob defended their guest.

"Mrs. Miller, I have never had a meal quite like this before. It was – well it was interesting. Thank you. I am afraid I still have chores waiting for me back home. Thank you for the invitation, Mam. Sir, I thank you for your hospitality." After a few more pleasantries, Jacob walked him to the door.

With a sigh of relief, Eben mounted his horse and headed for his family farm at the top of Walker's Hill.

"Hannah, it is a beautiful evening. Shall we take a stroll down to the river and watch the sunset?" Benjamin invited. "Abigail, please wash the dishes for Mother."

Benjamin and Hannah sat on the bench which James had built over thirty years ago overlooking the river. It was a tranquil refuge from children and grandchildren.

"Hannah, that was a lovely meal. But do tell me what is troubling you."

"What are we to do about Abigail?" she lamented.

"Why? Is she ill?"

"No. But she is practically past her bloom with no marriage prospects in sight!"

Benjamin laughed in relief.

"I am serious, Benjamin. You have spoiled her. She cannot cook or keep house. She is far too scholarly and intimidates every decent man who comes near."

"I would not worry about this. When she finds a man she loves, she will do what all ladies do."

"Which is?"

"She will let him think that he is smarter than she," he teased.

"Benjamin, I have no idea what you mean," she replied coyly.

"Hannah, sometimes I do not understand you. You are upset that Abigail is not yet married, but you were upset when Jacob did marry."

"Well, Jacob and Kate were awfully young."

"They were no younger than Grace when she married Micah."

"To be perfectly truthful, I had hoped our son would marry a more suitable woman!"

"Kate is a devoted wife and mother and a talented homemaker. She quadrupled the size of the herb and vegetable garden. She cooks and sews."

"She cooks weeds!"

"Those weeds are called fiddleheads. With a pat of butter and a pinch of salt, they are quite edible. Though I do admit it is an acquired taste."

"She castrated a cow!"

"It was a bull, dear. Personally, that is not a trait that I would look for in a wife, but in farming circles I understand that it is quite a virtue. Kate is a farmer's daughter married to a farmer."

"The way she lets those boys run wild, dirty and barefoot like little ..."

Benjamin put his arm around his wife in understanding. "Like little slaves running unattended on the plantation. This is Fryeburg. Even my prim and proper mother let us boys run barefoot throughout the summer. When you work on a farm you cannot help but get dirty.

Hannah, we do not live on a Virginia plantation, nor do we live in a proper Philadelphia boarding house. We live in a modest town of hard working farmers, artisans and merchants. You are a free woman. Our children and grandchildren are free to work and play, to go barefoot in the summer and to get dirty."

"You are a free man. I am an ex-slave. I will always be an ex-slave."

"No, you are a free woman who refuses to fully enjoy her freedom. You are only a slave to your past."

"To one degree or another, we are all slaves to our past."

"That may be true," Benjamin admitted. "Now that our children are adults, I think they need to know the truth about their heritage."

"Never!" she gasped.

"Do you fear they would not love you if they knew you were born a slave?"

Hannah stared at the river. "Sometimes truth is a heavy burden."

Eli thought there was no better feeling than to wiggle one's toes in grass warmed by the morning sun. He watched his mama tend the herb garden as Danny watered some plants in his own little patch.

"Elijah James," Nana called as she descended the back steps. Kate quickly looked up with a frown.

"Eli, have you ever seen such a beautiful garden?" Hannah smiled down at her grandson as she took his hand and led him to the nearby bench. "We are truly blessed that your mama is a talented gardener."

Eli beamed at his mother with pride.

"Do you know that when I was living in the big city of Philadelphia we never had a garden?"

The little boy's eyes widened. "If you did not have a garden, how did you eat?"

"We went to the market and bought food from other people's gardens. That is why I never learned much about how plants grow. Perhaps if you and your mama are not too busy, you could teach me a little bit about your plants."

Eli stood up tall and puffed out his chest. "First we have cooking herbs over here by the steps. We have oregano, dill, basil, chives, sage, rosemary and thyme."

"Yes, I am well acquainted with the culinary herbs once they are in my pantry," she smiled. "Old Nana planted these in her garden as well. She would give me baskets of them and I would dry them and store them. I guess I never noticed them when they were in the ground."

"I have transplanted these from my mother's garden," Kate explained. "Comfrey is used to make a paste to treat cuts, scrapes, burns and bruises.[4] This is a very important item in this family. Horehound and hyssop are used to ease coughs and respiratory ailments."[5]

"Then we have our plants to make tea. We have chamomile, mint, peppermint and lemon balm. I like peppermint tea the best. What kind do you like?" Eli asked.

"I am quite partial to chamomile, however I do enjoy a good cup of peppermint tea on occasion," Hannah smiled.

"Perhaps later this afternoon we shall have a tea party in the garden," Kate invited.

"You know when I was a girl in Philadelphia; all the houses were very close together sometimes they were even touching. We would drink our tea indoors for we did not have a pleasant yard with shade trees to enjoy.

Eli looked at his grandmother wide eyed in disbelief. "Where was the yard? Where was the grass?"

"Well, we did not have much grass. The road was just a few feet from the front door. They were not dirt roads, but they were made from cobblestones. In the summer the streets were so hot from the sun, you could never go barefoot or you would burn your feet."

"Do you mean to say that you never went barefoot?"

"Only the very poor who could not afford shoes went barefoot. Respectable people always wore shoes."

"Even when they took a bath?" Eli thought Philadelphia sounded like a very strange place with no grass, hot stones and people wearing shoes all the time.

Hannah chuckled. "Now that would truly be silly. People took off their shoes to take a bath and to go to bed. Decent people always wore shoes in public."

"I am glad that I do not live in Philadelphia!"

"Last night your grandfather explained to me that Fryeburg is not Philadelphia. In fact Grandpa's mother let him go barefoot in the summer."

"Old Nana is very respectable," Eli observed.

"I believe that I may have been mistaken. Perhaps young gentlemen such as you may go barefoot. However I expect that at dinner..."

"I know. Wear shoes and no wiggling."

VI

The Judge's Verdict

It was nearly bedtime one September evening, when Benjamin heard pounding on the back door. He immediately left his office and hurried to the kitchen where he found Hannah opening the door to Grace.

"Grace, what is wrong? Is it Mother?" Benjamin asked with concern.

"No, Mother is fine and sleeping soundly in her bed. It is Micah and Alden." She appeared embarrassed as Jacob, Kate and Abigail approached. "Benjamin, please come with me. I need a judge," she simply stated as she turned around and headed out the door.

Benjamin shrugged his shoulders to his family as he followed his sister-in-law back to the farm. "Grace, are Micah and Alden in trouble? Have the slave catchers returned?"

"No, it is nothing like that. Come with me to the kitchen."

Benjamin found two angry men glaring at one another across the Liberty Table.

"I want each of you to tell Benjamin your side of the story and then let him decide. I have had enough of this and I am going to bed," Grace declared icily.

"I fear I do not understand," Benjamin looked from his brother to his nephew as he took his childhood seat at the table. "Grace said she needed a judge."

"You are here to talk some sense into my son," Micah quietly seethed.

"I have told you, Father, my mind is made up and neither you nor Uncle Benjamin can stop me."

"That is a legal fact," Benjamin concurred. "You are an adult and no relative can stop you from making a decision. However, I am curious as to what has made my brother so upset."

"Uncle Benjamin, you of all people will understand. I am leaving the farm. I am leaving Fryeburg. There are no opportunities for me here."

"You mean, there are not enough taverns and loose women here," Micah interrupted.

"I understand that the conflict is Alden wants to leave Fryeburg and Micah, you want him to stay. I will ask each of you a series of questions. Just answer the questions and do not interrupt each other. Alden, why do you wish to leave?"

"There is nothing for me here. Life is so predictable. Every spring we plant. Every summer we water and weed from sunrise to sunset. Every fall we harvest and get ready for the winter. Every winter we freeze. Then in the spring we do it all over again. I have no future here."

"Micah, why would you want him to stay? You have both Jacob and Mr. Pierce to help you."

"Look what happened the last time he left home!" Micah hissed.

"Uncle Benjamin, you were a young man when you left for Harvard. Did you ever fall into temptation?"

Benjamin blushed. "I never had the opportunity. You see I have not inherited the Millers' rugged good looks for I favor the scrawny Bradford side of the family. For some odd reason the young ladies did not find superior skills in conjugating Greek verbs to be particularly enticing."

Grace could not hear the conversation from the bedroom, but she was relieved to hear loud laughter from the kitchen.

"I believe your father fears you will make the same mistakes. You have betrayed his trust."

"I admit I behaved very poorly. But I was much younger and foolish then. Grandfather said a man does not define himself by his mistakes. He learns from his mistakes."

"Your grandfather was a wise man. If you left Fryeburg, what would you do? Return to school? Work in Boston?"

"I am going to work on the Erie Canal."

"The what?" Micah forgot himself and interrupted.

"The state of New York is building a canal from Albany to Buffalo. Here, let me draw you a map. Here is New York City and the Hudson River goes up to here to Albany. They are building a 363 mile canal from Albany to Buffalo on the shore of Lake Erie."

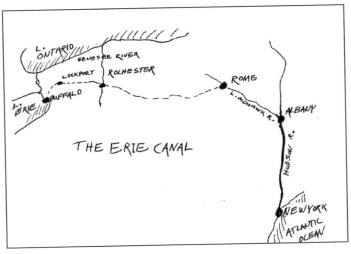

"That is impossible!" Micah gasped.

"A canal this large has never been attempted before." Alden grew excited. "The longest canal here in America is the twenty-seven mile Middlesex Canal between Boston and the Merrimack River. The longest canal in Europe is the one hundred forty-four mile Mili Canul du Midi in France. That is less than half as long as the Erie Canal will be.[1]

It will have eighteen aqueducts to carry the canal over ravines and rivers. Along the banks there will be a ten foot tow path for horses and mules to pull the boats."[2]

"I do not understand why horses and mules will be towing the boats," Benjamin admitted.

"The canal is only forty feet wide which is too narrow for sail boats and only four feet deep which is too shallow for steamboats with paddlewheels.[3] Special canal boats will be needed."

"According to your map, the canal will cross the mountains. How can water go uphill?" Micah was now enthralled with this feat of engineering.

"We will build eighty-three locks and climb an elevation of 675 feet."[4]

"What is a lock?" Benjamin asked.

"It is a chamber with gates on both ends. One of the gates is always closed. When a canal boat enters a lock, the closed gate is in front of it. After the boat goes inside the lock, the gate behind it also closes. If the next section of the canal is higher, then the boat must be lifted up to that height. To do that, water from upstream is allowed to drain into the lock, increasing the depth of the water in the lock and raising the boat floating on it.

Or, if the next section is lower, then water in the lock is released. When the water in the lock reaches the same height as the water on the next stretch of the canal, the gate in front of the boat is opened, and the boat comes out of the lock. This way, a lock safely carries boats to a different elevation, whether they need to be raised or lowered. Boats do not need to deal with rapids or waterfalls that a natural river might tumble over."[5]

"Draw me a picture," Benjamin requested.

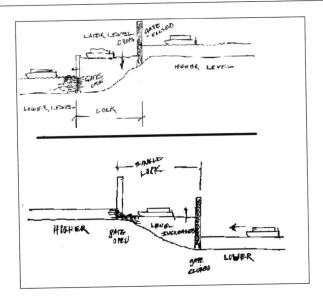

"This is unbelievable! Who invented this?" Micah asked.

"A man named Canvass White visited canals in England and studied their locks. His information helped the Erie planners design 83 locks, each 90 feet long, 15 feet wide, and 8 feet 4 inches high."[6]

"That is incredible!" Benjamin shook his head. "This will open up the west by cutting transportation costs in half."

"It is more like 90%," Alden corrected. "The farms further west can grow wheat and corn and ship them back to the cities along the coast. Textiles and other manufactured goods can be shipped west.[7] Right now it costs farmers $100 per ton to transport sacks of flour from Western New York, which has the ideal soil and climate to grow wheat, to Eastern New York where the major population centers are. After the canal is built it will only cost $10 per ton.[8]

They are searching for men with skills and experience in building canals. I met a man in Boston who is recruiting men to work on the canal. When I told him about my experiences in building the canal on the Saco River, he told me he could find a job for me. Well, he did!"

"There is no comparison between our little two mile canal and this project," Micah argued.

The Saco River meanders thirty-two miles within the boundaries of Fryeburg. The annual snow melts and spring rains flooded farmlands resulting in standing water, mud and erosion.[9] The lower section of North Fryeburg was called "Mud City". That area was not much above the river's level even at low water, and when the freshets came and flooded farms and houses the land was left in a sodden condition."[10] In March of 1815, approval was given to open a canal from the Saco River north of General Frye's Hill to Bog Pond running through the properties of Ebenezer Fessenden, Jr., Peter Walker, Isaac and Stephen Abbott.[11] One freshet finally caused the river to fill and enlarge the canal until the course of the river was permanently changed. Bog Pond and nearby Bear Pond were drained through the new canal. Yearly flooding in the North Fryeburg area was, indeed, greatly reduced. Alden worked on this project before he left for his ill-fated matriculation at Harvard College.

"Although I have had limited experience in canal building, I am still one of a few men who have any experience in building a canal at all. On July 4th 1817 they began digging near Rome, New York."

Glancing at the map Benjamin asked, "Why begin in Rome? That is the middle of the canal. Why not begin east and work your way west?"[12]

"The middle section from Rome west to Seneca is a remote stretch of flat land and the easiest section to work on. Since the crews have little to no experience in digging canals it made sense to begin here and learn as they go along.[13] They started out with 1000 men working on this 58 mile stretch of canal until winter and freezing temperatures halted construction. The following May 4000 men and 1,500 horses returned to continue the work.[14]

Things were going well until this summer as they tried to cross Montezuma Swamp where the mosquitoes were intolerable. Over 1000 men got sick and many died of canal shakes.[15] Many of the workers walked off the job.[16]

I suggested that they wait until the fall after the frost has killed the mosquitoes. Working with half frozen mud in the fall is better than dealing with the mosquitoes.

In October a 16 mile stretch between Rome and Utica will open up. Next year we hope to open the entire 58 mile middle section.[17] Even having this small portion open will be a boon to the local economy. There will be boat builders constructing line boats which carry freight and packets which carry passengers. Businesses will spring up along the canal. Loggers will use the canal to float timbers.[18] In addition to hiring Americans, we are hiring immigrants from England, Scotland, Wales Germany and Ireland.[19] People need to build camps to house all of these workers in the remote areas.[20] It is estimated that we will need to hire 9,000 workers by 1821.[21]

Next comes the fun part," Alden grinned. "We are going to work on the eastern and the western sections. We will need to build locks and aqueducts."

"You explained locks but what are aqueducts?" Micah asked.

"The Romans built aqueducts to carry water," Benjamin explained.

"That is correct. The canal cannot intersect with a natural waterway without being swept apart by the current. Therefore the canal will have to travel over the creeks and rivers on water bridges called aqueducts. Here, let me show you."

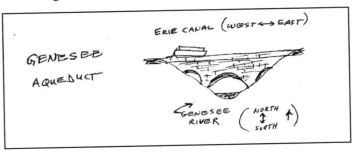

"We live in amazing times," Benjamin nodded his head.

"The largest one will span the Genesee River in Rochester.[22]

"Will building aqueducts be your job?" Micah asked.

"At the present. I intend to take the rest of Grandfather Peabody's inheritance and Libby's husband and I are going to buy waterfront property in Buffalo."

"Until today I have never heard of Buffalo. What is in Buffalo?" Benjamin grew curious.

Alden smiled. "Nothing much yet. But once that canal connects Buffalo to Albany, it will grow to be an important and prosperous city. Edward and I will open a boat building business. We will build canal boats as well as steam boats to be used on Lake Erie. With those profits we will build a trading post. Ten to twenty years from now, that waterfront property will be very valuable. When I sell it, I will become a wealthy man."

"You are a Peabody. Your grandfather would be very proud of you. Your great grandfather Peabody built a small boat building venture in Boston Harbor in the early 1700's and he amassed a fortune. Of course he and John Hancock were smugglers. I would not encourage that. However, boat building and business appears to be in your blood," Benjamin agreed.

Returning to his hand drawn map Alden illustrated, "See how close Buffalo is to British North America? It would be easy for a boat builder and merchant to frequent the Canadian border unnoticed. Smuggling appears to be in my blood. I could continue the Miller family avocation of transporting precious cargo to freedom. The future is to the west. There is no future for me here."

"Micah, I see your son not only has an immediate job offer, but long term goals as well. I left Fryeburg when I was seventeen in 1784 to follow my dreams and I returned to Fryeburg eight years later. I would have resented Father terribly if he had forbidden me to leave."

"You returned. But Ethan left nineteen years ago and he never returned, not even to visit."

"Father and Mother left their families behind when they moved to Fryeburg. Their families did not stop them. When you love your children, sometimes you have to let them go."

"That is easy for you to say. All your children and grand-children still live with you."

"Alden, when a man has a son, he has dreams. My dream was to someday have an office Miller & Miller Attorneys at law. When Jacob struggled in school and decided not to attend Fryeburg Academy I was devastated. After all, I was the first preceptor of the Academy and my own son refused to even attend. It took a long time but your grandfather helped me to realize that my job as a father was not to fulfill my dreams but to help my son fulfill his.

Your father spent his entire life on this farm, dreaming of the day that he would pass this legacy to you and your children. When you rejected this farm I am sure he felt that you rejected him as well. He lost his father, Sadie left and now you are leaving. You cannot expect your father to be thrilled that you have decided to leave him now.

Micah, it cannot be easy to be your son, growing up in your shadow. I know it was not easy growing up as Micah Miller's little brother. I could never measure up to you. You were always perfect – you were bigger than me, stronger than me and you never got into trouble. That was why you were always Father's favorite."

"Who me? I was certainly not his favorite! It was always 'my son, Benjamin, at Harvard' or 'my son, Benjamin, the attorney in Philadelphia' or 'my son, Benjamin, the pre-ceptor at the Academy' or 'my son the judge'. You were the favorite."

"Wait a minute!" Alden interrupted. "Are you telling me that the reason the two of you constantly bicker and argue is because you are jealous of each other? Does each of you think that the other is Grandfather's favorite?"

"Micah, off course you are the favorite! You inherited the farm!"

"Mother inherited the house and I inherited the land and barns. You hate farming. All you ever did was try to avoid doing your chores. When you finally did your chores, you complained the whole time. Why would he leave the farm to you? Besides he gave you the corner lot for you to build your house twenty-five years ago! You inherited his books. Do you hear me complaining that I never received a book from him?"

Alden started laughing.

"What is so funny?" Micah demanded.

"Both of you are wrong. Everyone knows that Uncle Ethan is the favorite."

"Now that you mention it, I believe you are correct," Benjamin agreed. "However, we digress. I will pronounce my verdict. Micah, I believe this is a history-making opportunity and you should give Alden your blessing contingent upon he leaves after harvest. Alden, you are now a man responsible for your actions. You can choose to honor your grandfather, father and your Heavenly Father, by your life or you can choose to dishonor them. The choice is yours. You are accountable only to God."

VII

Abigail at the Farm

"Be sure to write your mother," Micah reminded his son as he loaded the last trunk onto the back of the wagon. Alden would accompany Benjamin and Hannah to Portland where Benjamin would spend the next three weeks writing the new Maine state constitution. From there Alden would take a ship to Boston, then to New York City and another up the Hudson River to Albany. He would make his way west to Rochester to work on the aqueduct.

"Good bye, Old Nana," he dutifully kissed Sarah on her wrinkled cheek.

"I know you are a good boy, Alden and you will make your family proud. Your grandfather believed in you." She took his large hands into her small ones. "God be with you."

"Thank you. Mama, please do not cry!"

Grace wiped her eyes with the corner of her apron. "Be careful, Alden. This is dangerous work. Please write when you arrive in Albany."

"Good luck, Alden," Jacob shook his cousin's hand.

"Abigail," Alden hugged his youngest cousin, "I am counting on you to write to me because you know your brother never will."

Benjamin helped Hannah up into her seat. "Jacob, take good care of the house in my absence."

"Abigail, do try to help Kate in the kitchen," Hannah admonished. Abigail rolled her eyes and Kate smiled knowingly.

"Nana, please come home before bedtime," Eli pleaded.

"Elijah James, who is Nana's big boy?"

"I am!" he squealed.

"Well, you be a big boy and do not make your brother cry! I will not be home by bedtime. I will be home after the leaves turn yellow and red and fall on the ground."

With waves and shouts of good bye, the remaining family watched the wagon slowly make its way up the road and head toward Portland. Micah picked up a bucket, entered the barn and wiped his tears with his sleeve.

"Abigail!" Jacob rapped on his sister's bedroom door. "Abigail," he poked his head in. "Abigail, wake up. It is time for breakfast."

"No thank you. I am not hungry," she yawned and rolled over.

"I was not inviting you to breakfast. I am asking you to make it!"

She slowly opened one eye. "Let Kate make breakfast. She has been making breakfast every morning since Mama and Papa's departure."

"Danny was up half the night and Kate is feeling poorly this morning."

Abigail sat up in bed and groaned, "You know what that means. Not another baby! Will this house ever have any peace and quiet?"

Jacob grinned sheepishly.

"Aunt Abby!" Eli ran in and jumped on the bed. "I am hungry. Where is Nana?"

"All right! I shall make us breakfast," she snapped in exasperation. She had trouble coaxing any flames out of the dying embers in the kitchen hearth. Her mother made it look so simple.

Jacob entered the kitchen through the back door. "You are all set. I loaded the wagon with all the laundry and I will drop it off at Aunt Grace's."

"Laundry? What laundry?"

"You know, dirty clothes, dirty linens. Laundry."

"Why today?"

"Because it is Monday."

"So?"

"The second and fourth Monday of the month is laundry day. Mother always does the laundry with Aunt Grace and Old Nana."

"Since when?"

"Since before we were born. Mother says the key to performing unpleasant tasks is to enjoy good company while doing so. They do the laundry and enjoy the day together. Sadie is no longer here. Old Nana tries to help in her own way. You do not expect Aunt Grace to do our laundry for us, do you?"

"What am I, a slave?" she snapped.

That comment was like a slap in the face. "If you were my brother instead of my sister I would pound some sense into that arrogant head of yours!"

"If I was your brother, instead of your sister, I would be an attorney and I would not be expected to do the stupid laundry!"

A hungry Abigail walked up the lane on a carpet of pine needles to the farm. Jacob had already taken Eli in the wagon mumbling that perhaps Aunt Grace would take pity on them and give them some breakfast.

"Abigail, how lovely you will be joining us today," Sarah warmly greeted as Abigail entered the yard. Uncle Micah had set up the huge laundry kettle over the open flames. Eli was sitting on the grass contently munching on his third slice of cornbread. Aunt Grace was rubbing in some of her home made, soft soap into some stubborn stains.

"It promises to be a glorious day," Sarah, who was wrapped in her winter cloak and sitting in the sun, pronounced. "Look around. The leaves are at the peak of their glory."

Abigail hesitantly grabbed some sheets and looked around.

"We are doing whites, you can throw them in the kettle," Sarah explained. "Oh I received a lovely letter from your mother yesterday. She is enjoying her visit in Portland. Your mother was the answer to my prayers."

"She was?" Abigail asked in surprise.

"Your grandfather always accused me of spoiling your father. That was the only thing we ever argued about."

"I cannot picture you and Old Grandpa arguing."

"When two sinners marry, there are bound to be arguments. Your father taught himself to read when he was only four years old. After that he always had his nose in a book. Your grandfather gave him more spankings for not doing his chores.

I guess he took after me. I was a voracious reader as a child. My poor mother had a terrible time tearing me away from books to teach me my domestic responsibilities."

"I did not realize that you enjoyed reading," Abigail confessed. She remembered her grandfather was always reading while her grandmother was busy at the hearth or loom.

"There is a season for everything. I read copiously as a girl. When I had the responsibilities of running a home, I had little time to read."

"You have time now," Abigail pointed out.

"I have the time, but not the eye sight," Sarah lamented.

"I would be happy to read to you. I could stop by tomorrow," Abigail volunteered.

"Could you stop by tomorrow morning while I deliver my cheese and butter?" Grace asked. With Sadie gone, she did not wish to leave Sarah unattended.

Abigail respected her aunt for running the household and creamery while also caring for her parents-in-law. "Aunt Grace, I would be happy to visit any time you need." She threw more laundry into the kettle. "Old Nana, how was my mother the answer to your prayers?"

"Your father never had a friend his own age. Your uncles had much more in common and did not include him in their activities. Not that your father was interested in their activities. I fear after the death of his sister, he was a rather unhappy child."

Abigail could not imagine her successful father as a friendless, unhappy child.

"He only became unhappier when I arrived on their door step," Aunt Grace laughed.

"I fear your father felt Grace was usurping our affections and greatly resented her. She needed our love and understanding because she was very unhappy as well. It was a difficult time for all of us."

"I understand that Uncle Micah had much love and understanding for you, Aunt Grace."

"I admit I was flattered by his attentions. However I was convinced I would marry John Quincy Adams," she answered.

"Do you know President Adams' son?"

"My mother, your grandmother and Abigail Adams had been dear friends since girlhood. John Quincy would often come to visit with his mother and siblings when I lived in Boston."

"Old Nana, you were friends with the President's wife?"

"Yes, dear, we were life-long friends."

Abigail was incredulous that these two farmer's wives could be so interesting. "Aunt Grace, did you live in Boston during the Revolution? Did you see any British soldiers?"

"Yes and yes. Please help me wring out these sheets and hang them on the line. In fact forty British soldiers moved into our house and Mother and I were forced to move in with my grandparents."

"Your father's favorite past time was to read Abigail's letters," Sarah reminisced.

"You have letters from Mrs. Adams?"

"I have over fifty years' worth of letters. I remember when your father was so jealous of John Quincy Adams when he left for Europe and studied in Paris and Amsterdam. 'Nothing ever happens in Fryeburg' he would complain."

"Now I know where Alden got that from," Abigail pondered.

"Your uncle blames me for Alden's departure. I always told him stories about my family's ship building and trading businesses and how my father smuggled untaxed tea and gun powder back into the colonies."

"Now I understand why he wants to construct the Erie Canal, build boats and trade out west. Old Nana, may I read your letters from Mrs. Adams?"

"You cannot read them all in one day. Perhaps during every visit you could read a few aloud to me," Sarah suggested.

"Could we? That would be wonderful. But you never told me why my mother was the answer to your prayers."

"Your father left for Harvard as an awkward, shy young man. He returned from Philadelphia as a confident attorney. He practiced his opening and closing statements with your mother before his court appearances and practiced his lectures for Fryeburg Academy with her. She gave him confidence. She selected or made his clothing. She is a meticulous housekeeper and her home is always available to unexpected guests from the most humble farmer to the most important dignitary. She is his confidante. Why do you think she is in Portland with him right now? Who do you think coaxed him to become a judge?" Sarah smiled.

Abigail realized she knew very little about her mother.

"Did someone lose a little boy?" Joshua Pierce smiled as he rounded the corner with Eli sitting on his shoulders.

"I forgot all about Eli," Abigail confessed. How did these ladies do it all – cooking, washing, watching children?

"Aunt Abby, I was helping. I am a farmer, not a gentleman," Eli giggled.

"Uncle Micah is both a farmer and a gentleman," Aunt Grace explained. "A man can be both. Abigail, if you can finish the laundry I will begin the evening meal. Your family is invited to dine with us tonight."

"I am looking forward to your visits," Sarah patted her granddaughter's hand. "I regret that I have not spent as much time with you as with Libby and Sadie."

"I am looking forward to our visits too."

"Good morning," Abigail arrived cheerfully in Aunt Grace's kitchen with a book under her arm. This morning had gone more smoothly for both Kate and Danny were feeling better and breakfast was a calm and orderly affair. "Today I thought I would read *Rip Van Winkle* by Washington Irving.[1] We are a new nation now and we need to have our own authors and literature."

"I feel like a school girl at Fryeburg Academy," Sarah laughed.

"I will not be gone long," Grace assured Abigail as she packed up her butter and milk.

"Take your time and do some visiting," Sarah suggested. "I am in good company. Now shall we begin?"

"This is a light hearted story which I think you may enjoy," Abigail opened up the book to the short story of *Rip*

Van Winkle. "*Whoever has made a voyage up the Hudson must remember the Kaatskill Mountains*."

"The Kaatskill Mountains is where Alden will be working on the Erie Canal in New York State. How appropriate. Grace is so concerned about him. I know it is not easy to have your child leave home."

"I have never thought of that before. It must be difficult." Abigail continued, "*At the foot of these mountains was a village where lived a man named Rip Van Winkle, a simple good-natured fellow*."

"Do you know the Dutch settled New York? With a name like Van Winkle he must be Dutch. Keep going."

"...*The great error in Rip's composition was an insuperable aversion to all kinds of profitable labor*..."

"Your grandfather knew how to work! He built this home and established this farm and still had time to serve as church elder and town selectman. Never marry a man who is afraid of work!" Sarah admonished as Joshua Pierce entered with a bucket of water.

"Excuse me, ladies. I noticed the bucket was empty. This will save you the trouble of going to the well if you want to make tea." With a nod and a smile he returned to the barn.

"...*His children too were as ragged and wild as if they belonged to nobody*."

"That is a disgrace. It is the father's duty to care and provide for his children. I do not believe I care for this fellow."

"...*but his wife kept continually dinning in his ears about his idleness, his carelessness and the ruin he was bringing on his family*..."

"That poor woman! Did she not have the sense to see what kind of man he was? Abigail, it is better not to marry at all than to marry a man like that!"

"Yes, Mam. Please remember this is only a story."

"What is the point of the story? Does he repent?"

"No. He wanders off one day and fairies cast a spell upon him. When he awakes twenty years later he finds the world has changed."

"Fairies, indeed! That is sheer nonsense. I think it is time for tea. Remember my words, Abigail, marry an honest, hardworking man or do not marry at all!"

"Good morning, Abigail," Mr. Pierce opened the kitchen door for her the next morning.

"I just heard the most dreadful news!"

"If it is dreadful, perhaps you should not discuss it," Grace warned.

Abigail ignored her aunt's remark. "Did you hear about the landslide in Crawford Notch back in August?"[2]

Jacob cleared his throat and gave her a dirty look. "There was a terrible storm and the Willey family and two hired hands fled the house to seek shelter in their barn. The barn was buried in the slide and later people found their bodies in a mass of stone and rubble. The irony is the house was untouched. They found the family Bible opened and Mr. Willey's spectacles on the table. Why did they leave the house? If they had stayed home they would have lived."

"We should not question the sovereignty of God," Sarah admonished.

"We should not blame God for this tragedy. He did not force them to leave the house. They made a choice."

"Abigail, theologians have debated the sovereignty of God versus man's free will for centuries. You will not solve the problem this morning," Jacob glared at her. Joshua silently slipped out the back door and headed for the barn.

"Abigail, a lady should think before she speaks," Grace remonstrated.

"Mr. Pierce's family did not die in a landslide. They died in a fire. That is totally different."

"He blames himself for not being home that night. How could you be so thoughtless and discuss this tragedy in front of him," Jacob fought to control his anger.

"I will apologize." She entered the barn where she found Joshua combing Mike's mane. "Mr. Pierce, I have come to ask forgiveness for my thoughtless speech."

"Abigail, I know you meant no harm." He kept combing and did not look up.

"It was not your fault your family died. You should not blame yourself."

"I was detained on business in Danvers. Because of the late hour I decided to spend the night there and leave for Salem at daybreak. If I had come home that evening, I could have saved them."

"You would have died in your sleep with the rest of them," she contradicted.

"What do you mean?" he suddenly turned to her.

"Papa read me the newspaper article from Salem that reported they found your wife and children in their beds. They died of the smoke before the fire reached them. Think about it. If they had felt the flames, do you think they would have stayed in bed? No. They would have tried to escape. But their bodies were not found near a window or on the stairs. They died in their sleep. Mr. Pierce, you have the right to mourn the loss of your wife and children. But you do not have the right to blame yourself."

"Thank you, Abigail. I never knew that information."

"Old Grandpa said it is not the number of years lived on this earth but where you spend eternity that ultimately matters. Some may call the death of young children a tragedy. But a person who lives to be ninety-nine and spends eternity absent from God is a much greater one."

"Your grandfather was a wise man."

"What was your wife's name?"

"Her name was Helen. Our son Jonathan was four and our daughter Mary was two."

"What was Helen like?"

"She was very much like your Aunt Grace."

"You mean she was beautiful like Libby. Men always fall for a pretty face."

"Boys fall for a pretty face. Men can see a woman's worth behind the pretty face."

"You just proved my point," she laughed.

He deliberately changed the subject. "Will you finish reading Rip Van Winkle today? Your grandmother told me all about it."

"I fear I have upset her."

"On the contrary, she looks forward to your visits. I have noticed a cheerier disposition since you have begun reading to her. She talks about you all the time after you leave.

Sarah was smiling when Abigail joined her in the drawing room. "We received a letter from Alden.

October, 1819
New York City

Dear Family,

I spent two days in Boston with Libby while I waited for a ship to take me to New York. Sadie seems to be very happy and busy. She gives art lessons to children and adults. Her students certainly admire her. It is hard to believe but her painting is even more beautiful than before. She is working on three different paintings on commission. She often gets invited out to dinner by different families.

This afternoon I will take a boat up the Hudson River to Albany. I will write you soon.

Alden

"My parents came home last night. Papa was quite excited about the constitution. I am sure they will stop by and tell you all about it.

"It will be wonderful to have them home. What will we read after we finish *Rip Van Winkle?*"

"Perhaps we could read *The Legend of Sleepy Hollow*."

"Do you think I may like that story better?"

"I fear not. Perhaps I will read more of Mrs. Adams' letters instead."

Sarah sat in her chair alone in the drawing room staring at the menacing, gray November sky. The howling wind blew the few remaining leaves off the trees. Her arthritis told her it would rain today; the cold draft escaping through the window suggested it would snow. She wrapped her shawl tightly across her shoulders and shivered. Even with wearing her woolen petticoats and sitting near the fire she felt cold.

She glanced at her husband's empty chair and sighed. She dreaded facing another insufferably long, dark, cold winter. The tall clock in the corner struck ten. Time passes slowly when you have nothing to do.

"Good morning, Old Nana," Abigail greeted cheerfully.

"Mercy, child! Where is your cloak? You walked up here with just a shawl?"

"I did not realize it was so cold," she confessed as she warmed her hands by the fire.

Joshua entered carrying a load of firewood filling the wood stand by the hearth. "Good morning, Abigail. We did not expect you today," he smiled warmly.

"I came to read more of Abigail Adams' letters. Yesterday Mr. Adams was elected President and I have to know what happens next."

"I believe John Adams was elected in 1796, not yesterday," Joshua teased.

"Mr. Pierce, you are impossible," Abigail scolded good-naturedly.

"Everyone calls me Joshua."

"My parents call you Mr. Pierce," she contradicted.

"True enough," he conceded. "At the farm you may call me Joshua and Mr. Pierce at your house."

"Joshua, you may join us to the inauguration of John Adams," Sarah invited.

April 26, 1797
Quincy, Massachusetts

Dear Sarah,

My dearest friend and husband was inaugurated as the second President of the United States on Saturday, March 4 at the House Chamber of Congress Hall.[3] My own days have been taken up with keeping house, running the farm, settling issues with the hired men, managing the finances and caring for John's aged mother here in Quincy.[4] A few days ago Susanna Boylston Adams Hall died in the eighty-ninth year of her life.[5]

John Quincy is in love again, this time with Louisa Catherine Johnson, the daughter of the American consul in London. I do hope that she is the right woman for him and not too young or accustomed to the splendors and attractions of Europe.[6]

Tomorrow I prepare to set out for Philadelphia.[7] It shall be good to be reunited with my husband.

Fondly,
Abigail

"She missed the inauguration!" Abigail stated in disappointment.

"Sometimes family duties demand our allegiance." Sarah explained.

July, 1797
Philadelphia, Pennsylvania
Dear Sarah,

The task of the President is very arduous, very perplexing and very hazardous. I do not wonder Washington wished to retire from it. John is in his office in the President's House most of every day.

I am beginning to feel at home here as we have kept our old habit of beginning the day at five in the morning. Breakfast is at eight. We see each other again at dinner, customarily served at three. I am obliged every day to devote two hours for the purpose of seeing company.[8]

Today will be the fifth great dinner I have hosted. I expect about 36 gentlemen today, just as many more next week, and I shall have to get through the whole of Congress, with their appendages. Then comes the 4th of July, which is a still more tedious day. We must then have not only all Congress, but all the gentlemen of the city, the Government and officers and companies. I hope the day will not be hot.[9]

We will be leaving for Quincy in two weeks.[10] *It will be good to be home.*

Please write me at the Quincy address. I am eager to hear about the grandchildren and the building of Benjamin's house.

Sincerely,
Abigail

"Mrs. Adams knew who I am?" Abigail asked.
"She knew about all my grandchildren, dear."

103

October, 1797
East Chester, New York

Dearest Sarah,
John Quincy and Louisa Catherine were married on July 26 in London.[11] I look forward to the day I may meet my new daughter.

We left Quincy last week for Philadelphia. En route we learned that yellow fever rages again in Philadelphia and we have decided to stop and wait at the home of our daughter, Nabby. John is kept apprised by daily reports. Two-thirds of the population of the city has fled. The government has scattered to various outlying towns.[12]

"Who was running the country?" she asked her grandmother.

"I imagine the country can run itself," she smiled. "Abigail, it is snowing hard and the wind is picking up."

"Please let me read just one more letter. I want to hear about the day they moved to Washington."

November, 1800
Washington, D.C.

Dear Sarah,
It was an extremely arduous journey from Quincy to Washington. John had left weeks before. I found our son Charles in poor health and under the care of his sister Nabby in East Chester. I fear that I will not see him again.[13]

Woods are all you see from Baltimore until you reach the city, which is so in name only.[14] The immense house was still unfinished. It reeked of wet plaster and wet paint. Fires had to be kept blazing in every fireplace on the main floor to speed up the drying process. There is only a twisting back stair built between floors. Closet doors are missing. There are no bells to ring for the servants. Although the furniture arrived from Philadelphia, it looks lost in such enormous rooms.[15]

The house stands in a weedy, wagon-rutted field with piles of stone and rubble about.[16] *Yet, I can imagine that someday this white-washed stone edifice overlooking the Potomac River will be the largest and most gracious home in America.*

The weather is growing colder. I find it maddening that with woods everywhere, it is impossible to find a woodcutter to keep the fires going. I despair that anything can ever be accomplished in this society. Just yesterday I watched twelve slaves dressed in rags at work outside my window, hauling away dirt and rubble with horses and wagons while their owners stood by doing nothing. Two of our hardy New England men would do as much work in a day as the whole twelve.[17]

"You may wear my woolen cloak and run home," Sarah offered. "If the weather allows, you may return tomorrow and we shall continue."

"May I see you home? A lady should not be out alone in this weather," Joshua offered.

"Yes, you may if you promise to not read any more letters while I am gone."

"I solemnly promise. And a gentleman never breaks his promises," he smiled.

VIII

Merry Christmas!

"**M**erry Christmas, Aunt Grace!" Abigail greeted at the kitchen door.

"I hope you did not walk here in this frigid weather! It is only eight in the morning. Dinner will not be ready for another five hours!"

"Papa brought us in the carriage. We are bringing dinner," she handed two baskets to her aunt before pulling off her mittens and unwrapping her wool scarf which covered most of her face.

"Merry Christmas, Grace!" Hannah smiled and handed her two more baskets. "I cannot remember weather this cold!" she shivered. "Last night Benjamin and I decided that you have missed many church services while caring for Mother and Father. Our gift to you is we will care for Mother, prepare Christmas dinner and keep the fires burning so you and Micah may attend Christmas service together."

"I must tell you that is a wonderful gift! Mother is still in bed waiting for her room to warm up a little before she gets up. Abigail, perhaps you could warm her clothes by the fire and then help her dress. She may need her cloak as well."

Abigail found her grandmother buried under a mountain of wool blankets and quilts. "Merry Christmas," she greeted cheerfully.

Sarah Bradford Miller, like generations of Bradfords before her, did not "keep Christmas". Her ancestors separated from the Church of England to purify their faith. The Puritans rejected the notion of celebrating Christmas on December 25 because pagans celebrated the Winter Solstice in late December. It was the Roman Emperor Constantine who mandated this date for Christmas. The Romans celebrated *Dies Natalist Solis Invictus* the birthday of the unconquered sun on December 25 to celebrate the birthday of the pagan sun god Mithra. Early Christians gave this festival a new meaning, as they celebrated the birth of God's unconquered Son.[1]

She would never allow mistletoe or holly and ivy to decorate the house. Mistletoe was used by Druid Priests as early as 200 B.C. in winter celebrations. Ancient Celts believed that mistletoe had magical healing powers and could ward off evil spirits. Pagans also believed that holly and ivy had magical powers because they stayed green all winter. They would place holly and ivy over their doors to drive away evil spirits.[2]

Over the decades James convinced her that any time the saints would gather together to worship was always pleasing to the Lord. Sarah considered Christmas as another Sabbath to rest, to worship and to have the family gather for dinner.

"Mercy! This house is as cold as the barn," she shivered.

"I will warm your clothes by the fire first." Abigail then slipped the heated garments under the covers so her grandmother could get dressed under the warmth of the blankets. She helped her grandmother to her rocking chair by the fire where she brushed her long white hair, braided it, and neatly pinned it up. "You shall need your cloak as we walk through the hall," Abigail explained as she helped her to her feet and wrapped the cloak around her small, frail shoulders.

"Mother, have a seat by the hearth," Hannah invited as she pulled out a chair. You can keep us company and supervise us making the meal as Grace and Micah go to church.

"I am afraid we will be having Christmas dinner here. We could not possibly get the dining room warm enough for us." Grace was conveniently using her dining room as cold storage.

"As long as we are together, it does not matter where," Hannah attempted to sound cheerful and not glance as James' empty chair at the head of the table.

Grace already had the goose slowly roasting in the reflector oven. "I will begin making turnip soup. Mother and Abigail, would the two of you be so kind as to begin to pare these twelve turnips as I set the water to boil?" Hannah asked as she placed a pot with a half-gallon of water directly over the flames. She added eight pared turnips, black pepper, a whole onion stuck with cloves, three blades of mace, a half of a nutmeg, a mix of dried sweet herbs and a crust of bread into the boiling water.[3] "We will let that simmer for an hour or more. Now let us begin the winter squash."

Abigail and Hannah struggled to peel and chop a large blue Hubbard squash and placed the pieces in another pot with some boiling water. Sarah peeled and finely chopped three apples. Hannah placed the apples and a little water in a red ware bowl on a trivet over a pile of hot coals. Abigail drained the water from the cooked squash and mashed it. Sarah mixed three eggs, a cup of cream, ¾ cup of maple sugar, a tablespoon of rose water, grated nutmeg, a tablespoon of wheat flour and a small handful of bread crumbs. Hannah added the simmered apples into the mashed squash and then poured the liquid mixture on top and stirred well. She set this into a warm oven for an hour.[4]

"I made the quaking plum pudding yesterday. Now it is time for tea," Hannah announced. Abigail put the kettle on a trivet in the coals as Sarah dosed in her chair.

Micah, Grace and Mr. Pierce quickly entered the church and slid into the pew beside Jacob, Kate, Eli and Danny. "Please tell me that my father is not tending to the livestock," Jacob whispered to his uncle.

"Joshua did the barn chores this morning. Do you think I would leave my horses in the care of your father?" Micah replied.

The church was merely one quarter filled. The bitter cold kept many people from East and North Fryeburg home rather than risk frost bite on the long sleigh ride. Also many in the town were home sick with a variety of maladies. The sounds of muffled coughs and stifled sneezes filled the sanctuary.

The good Reverend Hurd, flushed with fever entered the pulpit. His family was also home sick today. "In the Old Testament book of Micah in the second verse of the fifth chapter, Micah prophesized 'But thou Bethlehem, though thou be little among the thousands of Judah, yet out of thee shall He come forth unto me that is to be ruler in Israel, whose going forth have been from of old, from everlasting.'

The old Puritans made a parade of work on Christmas Day, just to show that they protested against the observance of it. But we believe they entered that protest so completely, that we are willing as their descendants, to take the good accidentally conferred by the day and leave its superstitions to the superstitious.

I. First, then WHO SENT JESUS CHRIST?

'Out of thee shall he come forth unto me.' It is a sweet thought that Jesus Christ did not come forth without His Father's permission, authority, consent and assistance. He was sent of the Father that he might be the Savior of men.

II. Now secondly WHERE DID HE COME TO?

King David was born in Bethlehem and it became a royal city because the kings were brought forth there. But again there is something in the name of the place. Bethlehem has a double meaning. It signifies 'the house of bread' and 'the house of war'. Ought not Jesus Christ be born in the house of bread for he is our Bread of Life? If he is the spiritual food to the righteous, he causes war to the wicked. Sinner! If thou dost not know Bethlehem as the house of bread it shall be to thee a house of war.

Bethlehem is called 'little among of the thousands of Judah'. Why is this? Because Jesus always goes among little ones. He was not born in a palace in Jerusalem but a manger in Bethlehem.

We cannot pass away from this without another thought which is how wonderfully, mysterious was that Providence which brought Mary to Bethlehem at the very time when she was to be delivered. Mary and Joseph resided in Nazareth. Why would they travel at such an inopportune time? Because Caesar Augustus decreed there would be a census and Mary and Joseph had to travel to the city of their ancestors, thus fulfilling the prophesy of Micah.

III. This brings us to the third point of WHAT DID JESUS COME FOR?

He came to be ruler of Israel. Jesus Christ was said to have been born the king of the Jews.

Have you a Bethlehem in your heart? Are you little? Go home and seek him by earnest prayer. If you have been made to weep on account of sin, and think yourself too little to be noticed, go home little one! Jesus comes to little ones. He will come to your poor old house; he will come to your poor wretched heart; he will come though you are in poverty. Trust him, trust him, trust him; and he will go forth to abide in your heart forever."[5]

Reverend Hurd stood at the back door to wish each congregant a Merry Christmas. "Mrs. Miller, it is wonderful to see you in church this morning."

"It is wonderful to be here. Benjamin, Hannah and Abigail are staying with Mother Miller so we could make it today."

"How is she doing?" he asked with concern.

"You know my mother never complains," Micah explained, "but life is not the same without my father."

"Please give her my warmest regards and tell her as soon as I am feeling better, I plan to visit with her. Look how big Eli and Danny have grown!"

"I did not wiggle in church," Eli boasted.

"I noticed," the pastor winked before coughing again.

"Something smells 'licious!" Eli announced as he entered the kitchen and surveyed the many platters, pots and pans. "I am so hungry I could eat all of this myself," he declared.

"Everything looks wonderful," Grace smiled gratefully. "It was good to be back in church although there were very few there between the cold and sickness. Even Reverend Hurd looked quite ill."

"Kate, please have Daniel sit on this side of the table closest to the fire," Sarah instructed. "This is no time for him to catch a chill."

"But I want to sit by Old Nana," Eli protested.

"You can sit on the other side of me," she patted Eli's curly head. "There are two things I hope I live long enough to see. I want to see Joshua fatten up a little and I want to see Abigail married."

"Mrs. Miller, your two daughters-in-law are doing their share in that department," Joshua laughed and patted his stomach. I am sure young Mr. Walker will get over his shyness."

"I have higher aspirations than to be a farmer's wife," Abigail protested. Silence filled the room.

"I believe what Abigail meant to say was, just as her father would make a poor farmer, she lacks the attributes to make a successful farmer's wife," Joshua intervened. Abigail smiled at him gratefully.

The kitchen door opened. "Something smells delicious!" Jacob declared as he and Micah entered.

"How is the Hurd family?" Hannah asked.

"They were all home sick," Micah replied as he warmed his hands over the fire. "I will check up on them tomorrow."

"I am sure that we will have plenty of left overs for you to bring to them," Sarah offered. "I remember that terrible winter when my little Abigail and I were so sick. If it was not for Benjamin, I believe the family would have starved."

"Papa, you can cook?" Abigail asked in surprise.

"No. I can barter. I traded ingredients in exchange for cooked meals," he grinned.

"Your Aunt Abigail died the day before Christmas in 1780" Sarah explained to her grandchildren. "It was thirty-nine years ago, but it feels just like yesterday."

"Mother," Benjamin quietly spoke. "This family has celebrated Christmas during difficult as well as joyous times." He glanced at his father's empty chair. "But we are here together. Perhaps it would help to remember happier times."

"Of course," Sarah answered bravely. "Micah, would you please ask the blessing?"

He was no Biblical scholar like his father or an eloquent man like Benjamin. "Lord thank you for this food, this family and this home which You have provided. Thank you for Your promise of 'Blessed are those who mourn, for they shall be comforted. This family is in mourning and we need Your comfort. Amen."

"Old Nana, can we miss Old Grandpa while we eat?" Eli asked innocently.

"We most certainly may," she agreed. For the next fifteen minutes, the family spent passing food to one another and eating in silence.

"Oh Grace, I almost forgot," Micah said, "We received some mail yesterday that you may wish to read."

Grace eagerly took Libby's letter.

Dear Mama and Papa,

Edward and I are pleased to tell you that you will be grandparents once again this spring. I am in good health and it is wonderful to have Sadie with me at this time. All the children adore her! Susannah is showing a natural talent in painting.

Ten-year-old Eddie is Sadie's official escort. You know how she feels uncomfortable in crowds. She initially found the streets of Boston to be quite daunting to say the least. Eddie either walks with her or escorts her in the carriage.

The first Sunday, she found services at Park Street Church to be overwhelming. After Church Eddie approached Pastor Dwight and asked if he and Sadie could sit in the front row, so she could read his lips. Well Pastor and Mrs. Dwight have shown Sadie much kindness and several other church members have bought or commissioned paintings from her.

Three years ago, our City Mission Society started a Sunday school program to teach reading and writing to some of the poor children in the city. Because these children work during the week, Sunday is the only day where they can have any schooling.[6] Sadie has begun giving art lessons as well.

Sadie has many new friends and acquaintances, she is loved by the family and she is establishing a reputation and a clientele. I have never seen her happier.

Papa, I know how disappointed you were, when Sadie decided to stay in Boston. But if you could see how well she is doing. Perhaps we can convince you to come to Boston for a visit?

Give our love to Uncle Benjamin, Aunt Hannah and family. Please tell Grandmother that she is in our prayers and I tell the children stories about their great grandfather and her.
With love,
Libby.

Micah wiped a tear from his eye. "I also have another letter from Alden."

Benjamin tried not to shiver. Although the seats by the fire were comfortably warm, it was cold sitting across the table. Hannah had her wool shawl wrapped tightly around her shoulders.

December 1819
Rochester, New York

Dear Family,
I know I should have written sooner but I have been busy every waking moment. I met another canal builder named Henry Young on the boat in New York City to Albany. He and I are will be working on the aqueduct in Rochester.

I am in good health and staying warm. Mother, thank you for insisting that I take extra wool socks, hats and mittens. Working on a farm was good preparation for working on the canal. Some of these city boys cannot keep up. My only complaint is the food is terrible and I am hungry all the time. I miss eating meals with the family. Fortunately, there have been a few occasions when Henry has taken me to his home in Rochester. His mother and sister are good cooks and they pack plenty of food for us to take back.

During my first visit I learned that Henry Young is really Henrick DeJung. His parents were born in Amsterdam and immigrated to New York after they married. Pastor DeJung preaches in Dutch but the family is bilingual and speaks English at home. They have some strange customs. On

Christmas Eve they leave wooden shoes by the fireplace so Sinterklass ((that is Dutch for Saint Nicholas) will leave treats in their shoes.[7] There are many families of Dutch descent in New York State and Henry says this is a popular custom.

You can write letters to me in care of Henry's parents Mr. and Mrs. Wilhelm DeJung in Rochester. It might be several weeks until we stop by to visit, but you can be assured that I will get them eventually.

The house must feel empty with all of us gone. Give my love to Old Nana and ask Jacob and Abigail to write.

Your loving son,
Alden

Hannah was feeling very grateful that her little family lived together under one roof. "It must be a comfort knowing that Alden is eating Christmas dinner with a fine Christian family and Sadie is surrounded by her family as well."

"Also a package arrived for you yesterday. Joshua brought it upstairs for safe keeping," Micah smiled as Joshua left the warmth of the kitchen to run upstairs to fetch it.

"I am no artist, but I declare that this is a masterpiece!" Joshua handed Grace the oil painting of a ship docked in Boston Harbor. Everyone crowded around to get a closer look.

"That is truly breath taking," Hannah whispered in awe.

"I can smell the salt air and hear the seagulls just like when I was a little girl waiting for my father to return from sea," Grace sighed. "I do not believe it! Look! It is *The Amazing Grace.*"

Kate had never heard the stories of Grace's childhood in Boston during the American Revolution. Sarah explained, "The Amazing Grace was a nickname her father bestowed upon his precocious daughter. He had two ships, *The Sweet Elizabeth* named for Grace's mother and *The Amazing Grace.*"

"This ship brought home silk and porcelain from China, traded in the Netherlands, sailed up and down the east coast to New York, Philadelphia and Charlestown. I would spend hours standing on the dock with my grandfather waiting for this ship to return." Grace struggled to hold back her tears as she missed her father, father-in-law and her children.

Sarah took her hand, "Grace dear, today we will remember happier times. In a way this is a happy Christmas. My dear James is no longer ill or in pain. Libby has a beautiful family, Sadie is developing her God-given talents and Alden is working on the Erie Canal.

I know how difficult it is to let go of our children. I can remember the day Ethan left for Virginia. For weeks I would wander into his empty workshop and cry."

Benjamin and Micah looked at one another and simultaneously mouthed the word "favorite".

"But look at Ethan now. He is married with six children. His sons help him run his cabinet making business. He is doing the Lord's work. There is a time and a season for everything under the sun."

"Mother, what would I do without you?" Grace squeezed her mother-in-law's hand.

"Papa, are we going to stare at this picture all day or can we eat some plum pudding?" Eli asked in exasperation.

"Elijah James!" Kate scolded.

Sarah chuckled. "He sounded just like Libby. Remember how she would speak her mind?"

"I wonder where she got that from," Benjamin teased his sister-in-law.

Abigail turned to her mother, "Mama, I grew up hearing stories of Papa's childhood and stories of Aunt Grace when she lived in Boston. Why do you never talk about your childhood?"

Benjamin quickly looked to Hannah. She calmly replied, "Because I am ashamed of my background." Jacob held his breath. Would this be the moment? "You see I was born out of wedlock. My parents were married, but not to each other. It was not a happy childhood. When my father died at Valley Forge, Mr. and Mrs. Chase adopted me and took me to Philadelphia."

"Nana, is that the city that has no gardens and all the children wear shoes?" Eli asked.

Hannah smiled, "That is the very city."

"Mercy! The good Lord does not hold an innocent child accountable for the sins of her parents. There is certainly nothing for you to be ashamed of," Sarah pronounced.

"This is America. It does not matter who your parents are. It is what you choose to do with your life," Micah stated firmly. "My Grandfather Miller was a petty criminal who fled London to escape the law and landed in Boston. Yet I have never met a finer man than my father."

"Mother, as long as my grandfather was not King George, I think I could accept anything," Jacob joked.

"There is no danger of that," Hannah smiled with relief.

"That is all I need to know. May I please have more pudding?"

"Hannah, where would this family be without you?" Grace asked. "You are the sister I never had. Do you think Benjamin would have become a judge if you were not his wife?"

"The good Lord sent you to our family and no one or nothing could ever change that," she solemnly declared. Hannah looked at her family in gratitude.

A gust of wind violently shook the house. "It will be dark soon. I will clean up here. Benjamin, you need to get your family home," Grace warned.

It took ten minutes for everyone to retrieve their winter clothing from the cold hallway, warm them up by the fire, and get dressed before heading out the back door.

"Merry Christmas!"

IX

Parlor Stoves

It was late January when a wagon loaded with three large wooden crates pulled up to River View Farm. "They are finally here!" Jacob ran out of the barn.

"What is finally here?" Micah demanded.

"The parlor stoves that Father ordered."

Micah, Jacob and Joshua struggled to carry in the heavy crates into the house.

Abigail, who was visiting with her grandmother by the hearth exclaimed, "They are finally here!"

"What is finally here?" Sarah asked. "Mercy! What is it?" she asked as the men opened the first crate.

"Father ordered parlor stoves from German immigrants in Pennsylvania. These stoves made from cast iron plates use one third less wood than a traditional fireplace,"[1] Jacob explained. "He bought three stoves for our house and three for the farm. He was tired of having his ink freeze in the ink well every night."

"We thought you could install a stove in the drawing room, the dining room and Old Nana's bedroom," Abigail explained.

The men installed the first one in the drawing room and lit the fire. "I must tell you this is amazing," Grace marveled as the stove evenly radiated the heat. I can feel the warmth half way across the room.[2] A dozen people can sit comfortably within a large semi-circle instead of huddling near the fire. We can now have dinner parties in the dining room year round."

"My bedroom will be bearable in the mornings," Sarah gratefully added. "This is a miracle."

"Father says we live in extraordinary times," Abigail explained.

"Indeed we do," Joshua agreed.

The next day Sarah invited Mr. and Mrs. Weston, Limbo and Mrs. Osgood over to enjoy the warmth of the drawing room.

"This is most pleasant. The sunshine is streaming in and the room is warm," Mrs. Weston observed.

"If I did not see the snow outside, I would hardly believe it is winter," Mrs. Osgood agreed.

"Because we have been unable to attend church services this winter I asked Abigail to read some Scripture." She opened the large family Bible to the third chapter of Ecclesiastes.

"For everything there is a season, and a time for everything under heaven;
A time to be born and a time to die;
A time to plant and a time to pluck up what is planted;
A time to kill and a time to heal;
A time to break down and a time to build up;
A time to weep and a time to laugh;
A time to mourn and a time to dance;
A time to cast away stones and a time to gather stones together;
A time to embrace and a time to refrain from embracing;
A time to gain and a time to lose;

A time to keep and a time to cast away;
A time to tear and a time to sew;
A time to keep silent and a time to speak;
A time to love and a time to hate;
A time for war and a time for peace."

"A time to be young and a time to be old," Mrs. Weston joked.

Sarah responded, "Even to your old age I am He; and to hoar hairs will I carry you. I have made, and I will bear; even I will carry and will deliver you."[3]

"I have been young and now am old; yet I have not seen the righteous forsaken nor his seed begging bread," Limbo quoted Psalm 37:25.

"Abigail, never get old," Mr. Weston warned.

"But Sir, what is the alternative but to die young?"

"Job lost everything in one day. When you are old you lose everything slowly," Widow Osgood lamented.

"You slowly lose your vision," Sarah continued.

"And your teeth," Limbo complained.

"Feet? Limbo, what is wrong with your feet?" Mr. Weston asked.

"Not feet!" his wife said loudly in his left ear. "He said teeth."

"Limbo does not have any teeth," he argued. "It is difficult not to be needed anymore. Farming is a young man's job," Mr. Weston said sadly.

"It is difficult to be a burden to others," Sarah said softly.

"But you are not burdens," Abigail argued. "Look at what all of you have accomplished! Look at the families you have raised, the farms and businesses you have founded, the church you have built and the town you have established."

"Someday soon when we meet our Maker, none of that shall matter," Mrs. Osgood countered.

"When you are young you are distracted by the cares of this world. At our age, we have time to reflect upon eternity and to meditate on Scripture. If only I could have been this wise forty years ago," Sarah conceded.

Grace entered the room carrying a tray with her mother's silver tea service and set it down on the table by the window. "It is time for tea," she said cheerfully. Grace poured as Abigail handed the guests their tea.

"May we join the party?" Micah joked as he and Joshua warmed their hands by the stove.

"Tomorrow, I will bring some gingerbread," offered Mrs. Weston.

"That would be lovely," Sarah agreed. "Perhaps Abigail could read us that entertaining story of *Rip Van Winkle*. I should invite Mrs. Charles. She has rarely left the house since her husband died."

"Tomorrow, I will light the stove in the dining room and we shall eat in there. Perhaps Hannah would like to join us," Grace suggested.

The following Tuesday Reverend and Mrs. Hurd visited the six elderly congregants who now gathered around the warmth of the parlor stove. The good pastor preached a brief but loud sermon and Mrs. Hurd led the singing of A Mighty Fortress is Our God. He promised to return next Tuesday.

Abigail continued to read to the group. The ladies agreed that they preferred *Rip Van Winkle* over *The Legend of Sleepy Hollow.*

Once a house of mourning, River View Farm was now filled with companionship of friends and family five afternoons a week. Attendance peaked with ten guests and six Millers enjoying refreshments, stories, hymns, and laughter by the warmth of the parlor stove.

One afternoon Grace greeted her elderly guests, "I have just received a letter from Alden! May I read it to you?" Everyone eagerly took their seats.

Rochester, New York
February, 1820

Dear Family,
God created the rivers but the Irish built the Erie Canal.
Well at least the Irish thinks so. They are a hardworking,
hard drinking lot.

"I wish those Irish would stay in Ireland!" Mrs.
Charles opined.

"I guess the Irish have the right to move here just as
much as any of us," Mrs. Osgood retorted.

Grace continued, *Henry and I have been reassigned to*
a new project and we will soon be leaving Rochester. We
will be working on the Lockport Combine, seventeen miles
from Niagara Falls. This is an opportunity of a lifetime!
Remember when I was home and I explained how locks
would lift or lower a boat as the elevation varies?

Can you imagine water climbing a sixty foot high cliff? [4] *We*
are building a series of five pairs of locks in a row. Each lock will
have a lift of twelve feet instead of the usual eight feet and four
inches. They are built in pairs to accommodate traffic moving in
both directions. Otherwise traffic would be blocked up for hours.

Men are digging through three miles of solid rock – a
combination of dolomite, limestone and flint. They drill
holes in the rock and then fill each hole to the brim with
black powder and then press it down with clay. You light a
fuse and the powder blows up the rock.

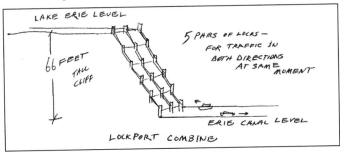

This is not ordinary gun powder. This black powder was just invented by a French immigrant named E.I. DuPont from Delaware.[5] This is very dangerous work. Mother, do not worry, for I have a very different job.

Henry and I have designed and built some cranes that lower buckets down to the heap of rocks. Men fill these buckets with rocks. Horses pull cables that swing the buckets up and away from the cuts.[6] So you see it is all very safe.

I will miss visiting Henry's family.

"What he means is he will miss Henry's younger sister, Gretchen," Sarah explained knowingly.

"I think we should write that young man a letter," Mrs. Weston suggested. "He must get homesick."

"If you have paper and ink, I will be happy to write the letter," Limbo volunteered. His eyes were still strong, his hand was still steady and he was rightfully proud of his fine penmanship.

"Be sure to mention the cold weather," Mrs. Osgood suggested.

"And the livestock," Mr. Weston added.

"And the sermon Reverend Hurd preached to us the other day," Sarah reminded. The next two hours were devoted to letter writing.

One evening as Grace helped Sarah into her bed she commented, "I believe this will be an easy winter."

Twice a month Hannah and Abigail spent Sunday mornings at the farm with Sarah and prepared the Sunday dinner freeing Grace to attend church with Micah. Abigail was setting the table in the warm dining room under the watchful eye of her grandmother. The kitchen door flew open with Eli and Danny exclaiming, "Nana, I am hungry. Is it time to eat?"

"Please hang up your coats in the hall and quietly take your seats at the table," she instructed as the rest of the family entered.

"Where is Benjamin?" Hannah inquired as she and Abigail brought the roast pork, butternut squash and potatoes to the table.

Micah rolled his eyes. "He will be here later and asks that we begin to eat without him."

Twenty minutes later an agitated Benjamin entered, hung his coat in the front hallway and took his seat.

"Mercy! Benjamin, what are you sulking about?" his mother chastised.

Eli and Danny stifled a giggle. Old Nana was scolding Grandpa!

"After all of our hard work, now this! We voted to approve to separate from Massachusetts in July. We wrote our constitution in October. We applied to Congress for the admission of Maine as a state. Now this?" he stabbed a slice of roast pork in the platter.

"What happened, Papa?" Abigail asked.

"When Alabama was admitted to the Union in December the nation was evenly divided into eleven free states and eleven slave states. The admission of Maine will upset that balance. Missouri has also applied for statehood as a slave state. Congress wanted to prohibit further introduction of slaves into Missouri and to free all children born of slaves already in Missouri at age twenty-five.[7] The Senate passed the Missouri statehood bill without any restrictions placed on slavery."[8]

"Missouri will be the first state admitted from the territory of the Louisiana Purchase. Are you implying that all of the Louisiana Purchase will have slaves?" Hannah asked in alarm.

"There is talk of limiting slavery in all the land beyond the Mississippi River to 36^0, 30" latitude."

"Missouri is north of that," Joshua contradicted.

"Except Missouri," Benjamin explained. "In December John Holmes from Alfred presented a petition to the House of Representatives asking for admission of Maine into the Union.[9] The speaker of the House, Henry Clay opposed the admission of Maine without the admission of Missouri as a slave state."

"Can they propose that both states be admitted together or not at all?" Jacob asked.

"There is no precedent for this. Previously each state was admitted individually," Joshua explained.

"What will we do?" Kate asked.

"Maine's admission should be postponed for a year rather than allow us to become a mere pack horse to transport the odious, anti-republican principle of slavery into Missouri,"[10] Hannah stated passionately.

"We should suffer martyrdom in the cause of liberty rather than yield an inch in favor of slavery,"[11] Benjamin agreed.

"I disagree," Micah interrupted. "Independence must take precedence over all other considerations.[12] We can fight slavery more effectively if we are a state rather than a mere district of Massachusetts."

"They are calling this injustice The Missouri Compromise," Benjamin sighed.

"Compromise, indeed! When righteousness compromises with evil, it ceases to be right!" Hannah proclaimed.

On March 15, 1820 Maine officially became the 23rd state admitted to the Union. While the town celebrated, Benjamin brooded knowing the country could not continue to be half slave and half free.

It was dawn when Hannah knocked on Abigail's bedroom door. "Please get up and pack some clothing. Jacob will take you and Elijah to the Farm to stay a few days," she said urgently.

"Why? What is wrong?" she sat up and rubbed the sleep out of her eyes.

"Danny has the whooping cough and we must get Elijah out of this house before he gets sick too."

Abigail could hear Danny's spasm of coughing which ended with a tell-tale whoop. Jacob was visually upset but remained silent when he tossed a sack of clothing into the back of the wagon and helped Eli and Abigail into their seat.

"Papa, why does Danny cough like that?"

"Whooping cough."

"How did he get it?"

"It is going around."

"Will I get it too?"

"Hope not."

"Eli, if we stay at the farm, away from Danny's coughing, there is a good chance you will not get sick," Abigail protectively put her arm around him.

"Will our baby get sick?"

Jacob turned to his son in surprise.

"I told Nana that Mama was getting fat. Nana told me she is having a baby soon and I should not call my mother fat."

"Your Nana is a wise woman," Jacob smiled. "Our baby is safe. Babies do not get sick before they are born."

"Is Danny going to die?"

"Your Mama and Nana are going to take very good care of him. Aunt Abigail and I had whooping cough when we were young and we did not die," he explained. He pulled the wagon up to the back door of the farm house, jumped out, grabbed the sacks of clothes and explained, "I am going to run in and let them know you are here."

A few minutes later Grace came to the door smiling, yet her eyes were filled with concern. "Eli, how nice it will be for you to stay with us. It has been a long time since Uncle Micah and I had a little boy living here."

"I am going to help Papa and Uncle Micah in the barn. Mama told me not to be a nuisance. I told her that I am going to be a big help."

"I am sure you will be. Uncle Micah can always use extra help. Come join us for breakfast first. A man cannot work on an empty stomach."

Abigail and her grandmother spent a pleasant morning sitting by the parlor stove reading more of Abigail Adams' letters.

Quincy, Massachusetts
April, 1812

My Dearest Sarah,

The year 1811 was an almost unbearably difficult and painful year. Our son Thomas was seriously injured when he was thrown from his horse. My sister was dreadfully ill and died on October 11, the day after her husband died of heart failure. Our daughter-in-law Sally, Charles' widow, was under the doctor's care for four months after she began spitting up blood. One night in September John went out in the dark to view a comet, tripped on a stake and ripped his leg to the bone. He was also confined to the house for months. Also on October 8 our daughter Nabby who is now living with us had a mastectomy.[13]

John Quincy and Louisa remain in Russia. Napoleon and the French troops are amassed at the Russian border. I fear that they will take Moscow.[14]

"The poor woman! I had no idea of the hardships she faced over the years," Abigail sympathized.

"Mercy!" Sarah exclaimed as she looked up and saw a smiling Eli standing in the door. "Elijah James, you take that raccoon out of this house this very minute!" she scolded.

Eli giggled, "Old Nana, this is not a raccoon this is Big Cat." He brought the large, long-haired, brown tabby cat into the room and placed it on her lap.

"His long, fluffy tail looks just like a raccoon's".

"He uses his tail like a blanket. See how his tail curls up and lies across him."

"He is a handsome creature, but you know the rules. People do not live in barns and animals do not live in houses."

"Uncle Micah says Big Cat is the best mouser he ever had. One night he even scared off a fox near the hen house. Now he is old and hurt his leg and cannot hunt. He will go hungry and die if no one takes care of him," he looked at his great grandmother with his big brown eyes.

"Do you have a touch of rheumatism too, old boy?" she asked while stroking his long fur. Her actions were rewarded with loud purring. "He is warmer than a lap blanket. Abigail, please give him a bowl of milk."

After lapping up his milk, Big Cat jumped onto Sarah's lap and promptly fell asleep. "Well, we still have an hour before lunch, please continue reading."

After lunch Reverend and Mrs. Hurd arrived with the rest of Sarah's guests. Big Cat opened one eye and with distained disinterest and fell back to sleep. Awakened later by the hymn singing, he silently leapt off of Sarah's lap and padded out of the room.

"It looks like he has adopted you, Mrs. Miller," Reverend Hurd teased.

"We have adopted each other," Sarah corrected.

Kate entered the pantry with confidence and determination as she gathered flour, molasses and lard.

"Are you baking?" Hannah asked.

"I am making a mustard plaster for his cough," she replied as she mixed ¼ cup of dry mustard and ¼ cup flour into a bowl. She stirred 3 tablespoons of molasses and added enough softened lard to form an ointment.[15] She dipped a clean flannel rag into a pot of warm water and wrung it out. Hannah followed Kate upstairs holding the damp rag and bowl.

Kate gently placed the warm rag on the feverish and listless child's throat and chest. She carefully applied the ointment on top of the rag being careful to not get any directly on his skin.[16] "Please check under the cloth in five minutes. The plaster can heat up the skin. The proper time for an adult is fifteen minutes. I need to be extra careful because he is so young. I will be back in a few minutes with a cup of tea."

Kate found the airtight stoneware jar which kept her dried horehound. She mixed ½ teaspoon with a tea cup of boiling water and let it steep for five minutes before straining the leaves out. She found Hannah peeking under the cloth on Danny's chest.

"His skin looks a little pink," she reported.

"That should be long enough," Kate replied as she lifted the ointment saturated cloth, put a clean, flannel cloth on his chest and bundled him up in blankets. "Depending on his cough, I will do it again in a few hours." When the tea cooled down, she helped her coughing son sit up and held the cup to his lips. "Just take a sip between coughs, Danny," she whispered.

Hannah admired Kate's expertise and calm demeanor. "Do you think he would be more comfortable if I rocked him in the rocking chair downstairs by the parlor stove? It would be warmer and he might breathe better sitting up."

Kate looked at her mother-in-law with gratitude. "If it would not be a burden."

"A burden? Not at all! That is what grandmothers are for. If you do not mind me saying so, you have very little room left on your lap," she smiled as she patted Kate's belly. "You get some rest. I will call you when I need you."

Before leaving the farm for the night, Jacob and Joshua brought a bed down from upstairs and set it up in the corner of the drawing room. "Eli, you and Aunt Abigail will sleep down here. Make sure you say your prayers and listen to your aunts. I will be back tomorrow morning."

"Yes, Papa. Can Nana come visit me tomorrow?"

"Maybe not tomorrow. She is busy caring for Danny."

"Is Grandpa taking care of Danny? Can he come visit me?"

"I will ask him," Jacob replied wearily. "Be a good boy."

When the tall clock in the drawing room struck eight Abigail announced, "It is time for bed."

Eli's lower lip began to quiver. "I do not want to go to bed by myself. I miss Danny! I want to go home," he cried. Abigail looked up helplessly to Joshua.

"If you go to bed without a fuss, I will tell you a bed time story," Joshua bribed.

Eli looked at him skeptically. "What kind of a story?"

"A story about a smart little girl who wanted to go to Fryeburg Academy when she got older but it was against the rules."

"What did she do?"

"You must get into bed for the night before I can tell you the story."

"I have to say my prayers before I go to bed," Eli explained. "I say my prayers with Papa!"

"I can say prayers with you," Abigail offered.

Eli gave her a doubtful look. "I want to say my prayers with Old Nana. She has more practice."

Sarah smiled, "That is true. I have prayed a lot with your grandpa and your papa. I guess it is a family tradition. The family bowed their heads and Sarah began, "Dear Heavenly Father thank you for bringing Eli to stay with us for a little while. Help him to know that you are with him and watching over him. Help him to not miss his family too much. Please be with Danny and help him to get better. Amen"

"Dear God, please do not let Danny die. I am very sorry that I called him names and a baby and made him cry. I promise when he gets better, I will never do that again. God bless Old Nana and Big Cat. Amen."

Joshua grabbed a lamp, "Off to bed for your story." Eli ran down the hall with glee.

After tucking Eli in and arranging his pillow he began, "Once upon a time there was a little girl named Abigail who was the smartest girl in the village school and had the best penmanship in Fryeburg. She was a shy little girl who loved to read. Fortunately for her, both her father and grandfather had many books and I think she read all of them.

Eli giggled. "The story is about Aunt Abigail. Did you know her when she was a little girl?"

"I knew her and your Papa when they were children. When I was a young lawyer just out of college I came to Fryeburg to work for your Grandpa.

Now one day little Abigail declared, 'When I get older I am going to go to Fryeburg Academy.' But her older brother teased her, 'You cannot go to Fryeburg Academy. Only boys can go'."

"Did Papa tease her a lot?"

"I think all big brothers tease their younger siblings. I had six big brothers and they teased me all the time. I think that is why I became a lawyer. I learned to defend myself at a young age," he laughed.

"Why do big brothers tease their little brothers?"

"Maybe they are jealous. You know babies are pretty helpless and they need a lot of attention. Maybe it makes them feel important."

"Will our new baby need lots of attention?"

"All babies do."

"Will Danny be jealous?"

"Probably. But you can teach him how to be a big boy and spend time with him."

Eli gave that some thought. "How did Aunt Abigail go to Fryeburg Academy if it was against the rules? Did she break the rules?"

"Your grandfather changed the rules."

Eli yawned and said, "Grandpa is a 'portant person." Then he fell asleep.

With an overwhelming sense of loneliness for his own son, he covered the sleeping child with an extra blanket.

Abigail witnessed the tender scene with gratitude. "Thank you," she whispered. "I did not know what to do."

"Well, I have had practice," he replied sadly.

The next morning Benjamin arrived at the farm carrying his leather satchel and found the ladies sitting in the drawing room. Grace was sewing as Abigail was reading aloud. "Mother, who is your friend?" he asked cheerfully as he pointed to the large cat draped over her lap.

"This is Big Cat and we are taking care of each other for a while."

Eli came running in, "Grandpa, did you miss your big boy?"

"Everyone misses you and they are taking good care of your brother. It will be a while before Danny feels better. I brought you something," Benjamin reached into his satchel.

"They are books," he said disappointedly as he surveyed the old blue back speller, the New England primer and a slate.

"These are not just any books," Benjamin corrected. "Old Nana taught my brothers and me with these books. Nana and I decided that Aunt Abigail will spend an hour each day teaching you your letters and spelling words."

"Grandpa, I am five years old. I do not have to go to school until I am seven. The sap is running and we are going to tap the maple trees. I am afraid I do not have time for this."

"You will make time for this, young man. Beginning tomorrow after breakfast, you and Aunt Abigail will spend an hour together. When you are through, you may spend the rest of the day working on the farm with Uncle Micah," Benjamin replied sternly.

"Yes, Sir. May I go out now?" He kissed Old Nana on the cheek, and patted Big Cat good bye and ran out the door.

"That child is better than medicine," Sarah laughed. "Before you go rushing back to your office, stay for a cup of tea."

"I am sorry, Mother. I am afraid I do not have time."

"You will make time, young man!" she reprimanded as Grace and Abigail tried not to laugh.

It was almost dark when Eli returned to the house exhausted, hungry, and cold. "Aunt Grace, I helped carry the pails to the trees," he bragged.

"He is the hardest working five-year-old I ever met," Joshua admitted.

"I am going back home now," Jacob turned to his son. "Be... "

"I know – be good, say your prayers, listen to Aunt Abigail, go to bed. Mr. Pierce will tell me another bed time story tonight."

Jacob looked at his relatives with gratitude. "I do not know how to thank all of you."

There were no bedtime stories that evening. The exhausted Eli tumbled into bed around 7:30 and fell fast asleep.

"If you excuse me, I have some paper work to do for Mr. Miller," Joshua lit an oil lamp and took a seat in the quiet dining room.

Abigail followed him." I always help Papa with his paper work in the evenings. That is my job!" she said crossly.

"Have a seat," Joshua calmly pointed to the chair beside him and spread the papers out on the table. I will help you put Eli to bed at night and you may help me with these wills and deeds."

"Why would he ask you to do this? This is my job."

"There will always be wills and legal work to do, but you have more important responsibilities at the moment. Your father has hired me to assist him. If you wish to discuss this matter with him, that is your prerogative. However, I need to get this done by morning. You may choose to help me or leave me be."

She glared at him. "I would be pleased to help."

It was mid-April when Danny had recovered and Eli was to return home. "Old Nana, I will miss you," he tearfully hugged his great grandmother.

"Mercy, child! You live a half mile up the road. You may come and visit Big Cat and me anytime you wish. You know your Mama will be having that baby sometime soon. You can stay with us for a few days then. Mr. Pierce will take you and Aunt Abigail home. Now pack up your clothes and books," she instructed.

Joshua was waiting for Abigail in the barn. "May we talk?"

"I will not object if Papa continues to hire your services."

"That is not what I wish to speak of. When I was at Mr. Evans' tannery yesterday I heard that Eben Walker is engaged to be married to Betsy Abbott after the harvest.

"Well, they are well suited for one another," she nodded.

"I am sorry, Abigail. Are you disappointed?"

"Truthfully, I am relieved."

"Joshua, I wish to speak to you," Sarah pointed to the chair next to hers. Even though it was late April, Sarah insisted on keeping the parlor stove going in the drawing room. He hesitated. "This shall not be long.

For years I blamed myself for my daughter's death. If only I had taken better care of her. If only I had called for the doctor sooner. If only I had not been sick myself. I was so consumed with guilt, I could not be grateful for what I had. One day I decided to stop blaming myself and then something worse happened. If I was not at fault then who was? God could have healed her. He could have prevented her death. Why did He not intervene? My guilt only disguised my anger at God.

Are you shocked that I was angry at the Almighty? When I admitted this to myself, somehow I began to feel better. I mean the Good Lord certainly knew I was angry at Him, so why pretend?

Joshua, it has been three years. You will always remember and love your family. It is time to confess you are angry at God and need His comfort so you may begin to live the rest of your life."

"Yes, Mam," he stood up and left. For the first time that night, he cried himself to sleep.

Kate was exhausted when she fell into bed. Not even the twinges in her expanding belly would keep her awake tonight. By experience she knew that she would deliver her third child sometime tomorrow.

Her brothers called her the mid-wife of the barn yard because as a child she was always present when the horses would foal or the sheep would lamb. Later as a young woman she accompanied her mother to attend her sisters-in-law's deliveries. The births of her two sons were uneventful. Yet Kate felt apprehensive.

At midmorning the next day Hannah asked, "Abigail, please bring both boys to the farm and ask Aunt Grace to come quickly," she smiled. "It is time."

"Should I get Jacob?"

"Leave your brother be. He will only be a nuisance. Your father has left to get Mrs. Wiley. Kate will have all the comfort she needs. Now grab your shawl and be off."

When Jacob spied his sister and sons walking to the farm he turned to Joshua, "I think it is time."

Joshua slapped him on the back.

"We will keep you busy to make the day pass quickly," Micah recalled his own excitement and apprehension each time Grace delivered.

It was late afternoon when Abigail entered the barn. "Papa would like to speak with you in the dining room," she stated solemnly.

Jacob turned pale as he left.

"Have a seat, son," Benjamin pulled out a chair.

"Katie! Is Katie all right?" he asked as he remained standing.

"Your wife is in good health," Benjamin assured.

"The baby!" Jacob gasped as he ran out the door and up the lane to his house. "Katie!" he called as he burst into the kitchen and ran up the back staircase two steps at a time. He found his wife in bed propped up with pillows nursing the infant.

"She is perfect," Kate whispered as tears streamed down her cheeks.

"We have a daughter?" he smiled. "Is it our Rachel?" for that was the chosen name if the child was to be a girl.

"Katie, I do not understand. Father..." For the first time he noticed his mother silently sitting in the corner holding a small bundle wrapped in a blanket. "Mother?" he crossed the room and peered into the blanket.

"Her name is Rebecca," Hannah handed the tiny, still-born infant to her son.

"Rebecca," he whispered.

It was mid-June and the lilacs were in full bloom. Kate found Old Nana sitting in her chair looking out the window at the newly tilled fields. There was no fire in the parlor stove. "Let me hold that precious child," she beamed. Kate carefully placed the sleeping infant in her great grandmother's loving arms. "She is beautiful. Welcome to the family, little Rachel," she cooed. "How are you doing, Kate?" Sarah asked in concern.

"The children are keeping me busy," she tried to smile.

"Do you know that I once had twins? I lost my Abigail when she was twelve. I also had a husband and three children to keep me busy but my heart was still broken. It will take time. You will always love and remember her. Things take time."

Kate was grateful that Sarah understood her pain.

"James never understood why I needed to visit Abigail's grave as often as I did. I can no longer go to the cemetery. When you put flowers on Rebecca's grave, will you also put some on my Abigail's as well? If anyone should discourage you from going just tell them that Old Nana sent you."

X

The Visit

It was the four year anniversary of the death of Rebecca Miller. Kate, accompanied by her four-year-old daughter Rachel, placed a bouquet of forsythia on the grave of the first Abigail Miller before stopping in front of a tiny slate headstone reading:

Rebecca Katherine Miller
Beloved daughter of Jacob and Katherine Miller
May 4, 1820 – May 4, 1820

After paying their respects Kate and Rachel headed back home when they were greeted by nine-year-old Eli and seven-year-old Danny leaving the Village School. The four stopped to let a large wagon filled with people and trunks pass before crossing the street.

"Papa!" Abigail ran into her father's office without knocking. "I could swear that I saw Uncle Micah all dressed up, an unfamiliar woman, young boy and Cousin Libby heading toward the farm."

Benjamin smiled broadly. "That was not Uncle Micah. That was Uncle Ethan." Benjamin ran out of his office calling, "Hannah! Ethan has arrived."

It was a warm May afternoon and Micah was restless. It was too early to plant, his winter chores were completed and maple season ended weeks ago. He was leaving the barn when he heard the wagon approaching.

Ethan Miller was astounded on how Fryeburg had changed since 1800! It was no longer a small village and scattered farms. His father and most of the old timers were gone; grandchildren and great grandchildren had been born. The many newcomers in town had not recognized him as he passed. As he approached the farm he thought he saw his father standing in the door yard awaiting his return after a twenty-four year absence.

"Welcome home! It is good to see you," Micah greeted with a hearty slap on the back.

Ethan embraced his oldest brother. It is good to be back!" He helped his fashionably dressed wife down from the wagon. "Olivia, I want you to meet my brother, Micah."

"It is a pleasure, Sir," she said with a southern drawl.

"This is our youngest son, Asher," he helped the pale and small ten-year-old down from the wagon. "This is your Uncle Micah." The boy smiled shyly. "Asher wants to be a lawyer."

"Heaven help us!" Micah laughed. "Is not one lawyer in the family enough?"

"Of course, you know this young lady," Ethan smiled.

"Hello, Papa. I have come home."

"Sadie! Sadie!" he embraced her in a bear hug.

"Welcome home, Sadie. Your family has missed you," Joshua greeted. He outstretched his hand to shake Ethan's. "Joshua Pierce. I am a farmer by day and lawyer by night."

Grace ran out the back door, "Sadie! What a surprise! Look at you." Sadie was dressed in a gray silk, empire waist dress, with a silver necklace. Her hair was pulled up with cascading curls falling to the nape of her neck. Grace held her daughter as if she never intended to let go.

"Where are my manners? You must be Olivia," Grace felt self-conscious wearing an old shift, her work skirt and apron. "We have enjoyed reading your letters over the years. We have so much to talk about! How long can you stay? This must be Asher. You look just like your father. Please come in and we will get you settled."

"How is mother?" Ethan asked with great concern.

"She is failing fast. She will be so pleased to see all of you," Grace answered wearily.

Ethan quietly entered the drawing room and was shocked to see a frail, elderly lady asleep slumped in his mother's wingback chair. An old fluffy cat curled up on her lap. He gingerly walked up to her and knelt in front of her chair.

"Mother?"

Sarah's eyes flew open.

"Do you remember me?"

A look of recognition crossed her face as she smiled. "Oh James, you have come back for me. I knew you would not leave me behind forever."

"Mother, it is Ethan," his voice choked. "I am sorry, mother, for not coming sooner."

"Ethan! My eyes are not what they were. And you must be Olivia."

"Yes, Mam. It is indeed a pleasure to finally make your acquaintance."

"This is our youngest son, Asher." Ethan introduced the young boy who quietly stood by his father's side.

Sarah looked across the room. "Mercy! Libby what are you doing here?"

"I am Sadie, not Libby."

"My eyes are not good. Come here so I can get a look at you. Sadie, I have missed you! I was afraid that I would never see you."

"I missed you too," Sadie cried. "I promise I will not leave you again."

"Look at you all dressed up like a fine lady."

Sadie laughed. "These are my fancy, Boston clothes. I have had several art shows and Libby insists that I wear a new dress to each one. Libby says, 'There is a time for farm clothes and a time for city clothes.' As soon as I go upstairs I will put on my farm clothes. Then you will recognize me."

"I want to hear all about Boston. Now have a seat," Sarah motioned to James' wingback chair.

"At first I found Boston to be over whelming. Libby's oldest son Eddie served as my official escort showing me the city until I gradually learned my way. I discovered I enjoy teaching art and giving painting lessons. Eddie was my first student. When Libby's friends learned I gave lessons, they enrolled their children in my art classes.

I love the smell of the salt water and the feel of the sea breeze on my face. I think I have mastered the art of painting water. Eddie would direct me to the most fascinating locations on the waterfront. He and I would paint together for hours.

I also painted several murals in some of the grandest houses I have ever seen. However I prefer painting on canvas. I met many interesting people. I am not quite sure if I liked them all. Libby dragged me to endless dinners and teas to socialize with prospective patrons. After a while I found them to be tiresome, but the food was always good.

Tomorrow I shall discuss with the headmaster at the academy about teaching painting to the young ladies this summer."

"To think I will have two granddaughters teaching at Fryeburg Academy!"

"I would like your permission to give lessons here in the drawing room."

"Permission shall be granted if I may stay and watch," Sarah smiled. "I believe I need a short rest before supper. Please help me to my special chair. Last year Joshua added wagon wheels to an old wooden chair. Is he not clever? Even Eli can safely wheel me from room to room."

It took the new arrivals over an hour to get settled in their rooms upstairs. Sadie's bedroom was just as she left it. However, Ethan was dismayed that Joshua Pierce had moved into his childhood bedroom and he and Olivia moved into Libby's old room.

Grace was busy setting the dining room table with her mother's finest linen table cloth and china imported from London. Back in 1781 Grace had removed the contents of her parents' Boston mansion and shipped them to Fryeburg.

Benjamin and his family arrived with baskets of fiddle-heads, asparagus, bread and a jug of hard cider. "We thought you may need these to augment your unexpected dinner party," Hannah offered.

"Oh Hannah, what would I do without you?"

"You mean what we would do without each other?" she corrected. "We will share the hospitality by having them over for supper each evening."

Ethan and Asher came downstairs first. "Asher, I would like to introduce you to the Honorable Benjamin James Miller."

"It is an honor to meet you, Sir," The young boy quietly responded.

"Call me Uncle Benjamin," he smiled as he shook the boy's small hand.

"Asher wants to be a lawyer," Ethan explained.

"Finally another Miller wants to be a lawyer!" Benjamin laughed. "It is indeed a pleasure to make your acquaintance, young man." Asher decided he would like this new uncle.

"Now let me introduce you to your cousins. This is my son, Jacob."

"Look at you all grown up!" Ethan exclaimed.

"Grown up with a wife and family," he added. "May I introduce you to my wife, Katherine Wiley Miller, my sons Elijah and Daniel and my daughter Rachel? You must be Asher. I am sure Eli and Danny will be thrilled to have another boy in the family to play with."

Asher felt uneasy about playing with these robust farm boys but politely responded, "Yes, Sir."

"Is this little Abigail? Asher, Abigail is a teacher at Fryeburg Academy and assists Uncle Benjamin in his office."

All the women Asher knew back home were seamstresses or wives and mothers. This side of the family was proving to be quite interesting. The sound of rustling skirts announced that Olivia and Sadie had descended the stairs.

"Sadie, welcome home! Everyone has missed you!" Hannah embraced her niece.

"Do you have any new paintings to show us?" Benjamin asked slowly and distinctly so his niece could read his lips.

She smiled, "I have a few left. But I sold most of them."

"Olivia, welcome to Fryeburg. I am delighted to finally meet you. This is my wife, Hannah."

Olivia studied the dignified woman attired in a simple but elegant dress, with black curly hair streaked with silver and olive complexion. "Hannah could not possibly be .... Could she?"

"After years of reading your delightful letters, it is wonderful to finally meet you," Hannah greeted cordially. "I believe Mother is up from her nap and we shall proceed to the dining room."

Hannah wheeled Sarah to the foot of the table as the family crowded around. Ethan was annoyed that Joshua Pierce was now sitting in his childhood seat with Abigail sitting comfortably beside him.

Ethan silently surveyed the scene before him. Micah sat in his father's seat at the head of the table. Apparently the rest of the family failed to notice that Grace's table cloth was faded and thread bare and there were a few chips in the china. Hannah quietly sat beside Sarah, cutting up her food and feeding her the small pieces. He no longer felt like part of this family. He was an invited guest observing them from the outside.

"How long will you be visiting?" Benjamin broke the silence as the family was busy passing platters of food.

"We hoped we could stay until October. Asher's doctor suggested that the clear mountain air would be healthier than the heat and humidity in Virginia. Now the boys are old enough to run the furniture shop and our oldest daughter, Maggie can manage the dress shop. Mother, I deeply regret we were not able to visit before Father died."

"Ethan, you are a man with responsibilities. He died knowing that his three sons were successful," she consoled.

"Benjamin, we were wondering if you would be available to tutor Asher in Greek and Latin," Olivia asked hesitantly.

"I will be in court the rest of the week, but Abigail can begin language lessons tomorrow morning."

"I shall be delighted. What grade are you in school?"

Asher looked uncomfortable. "I am not able to attend school. I tend to get sick a lot. I have a tutor when I am well enough."

"I was rather sickly myself," Benjamin sympathized. "My parents taught us at home."

Eli was uncertain if he should pity his sickly cousin or envy him for the freedom from school attendance. "After we eat, Danny and I will take you down to see the river," he invited.

"Oh, I do not know if that would be wise," Olivia responded protectively as she looked to Ethan.

"I think evenings by the river is just what the doctor ordered," Ethan encouraged. "He will be fine, Dear," he patted Olivia's hand. "In fact I think I would like to visit my father's grave tonight."

"We ladies will visit while you are out," Hannah smiled. We will take our tea in the drawing room. Would you like that, Mother?" Sarah was quietly dozing in her chair.

Danny and Eli walked very slowly so Asher could keep up. "How old are you? What is Williamsburg like? Did you like sailing on a ship? Did you like Boston?"

Asher was flattered by the attention because his older siblings at home ignored him. After taking a brief rest they made it to the river. Eli attempted without success to teach Asher how to skip stones across the water.

"We have all summer to practice," Danny reassured.

Micah, Ethan, Benjamin and Jacob headed down the road to Main Street.

"The family does not know," Ethan blurted. "I have never told them about my activities in helping slaves come north to freedom. I have to protect them."

"That must be very difficult for you," Benjamin sympathized.

"I have had a few close calls and some people are growing suspicious. It is time to make arrangements for someone else to take over my responsibilities. I have a friend who I can trust."

"What about George's mother and sister?" Jacob asked with concern. "We promised him five years ago we would get them out."

Ethan shook his head. "A few months after George left, his mother Ella broke her leg. It did not heal properly and she walks with great difficulty. There is no way she could make the journey. George's sister, Millie, refuses to leave without her. When Ella's owner talked about selling her, I convinced Olivia to take her into the dress shop. Ella can sew sitting comfortably in a chair and Olivia pays Ella's wages to her master."

"Uncle Ethan, we are supposed to free slaves, not hire them," Jacob argued.

"Everything is always black and white with you northerners," he snapped. "It is the best I can do in an imperfect world to keep mother and daughter together."

"Ethan, you are a brave and honorable man. Those of us living in Maine cannot appreciate the situation you are in," Benjamin consoled. "You need not explain yourself nor apologize to us." The four men silently walked into the village cemetery and stood in front of James's grave.

"I cannot believe he is gone. I have imagined home and Fryeburg to be just as I left it over twenty years ago. I feel like..."

"Rip Van Winkle," Jacob laughed.

Hannah and Abigail made tea while Grace and Sadie helped Sarah into bed. Big Cat was waiting expectantly on the pillow. Abigail loaded a pewter tray with teapot, cups and sauces and brought them out to the drawing room.

"I am most grateful that Sadie has returned home. It now takes two people to get her in and out of bed," Grace explained wearily.

"Aunt Grace, I will be over tomorrow morning," Abigail reminded. "After my Latin and Greek lessons with Asher, I will be free to stay and help."

"Abigail, where did you learn Greek and Latin?" Olivia initiated the conversation.

"Father taught me in his spare time."

These Miller women were an exceptional lot. Abigail was an instructress at the local academy and Sadie was a successful painter. Olivia had visited Libby and her family in Boston in their spacious home on Beacon Hill. Clearly Libby inherited Grace's charm and beauty.

"Now I have heard the stories of the Peabodys of Boston and how Grace arrived unexpectedly to Fryeburg. Hannah, were you born in Fryeburg or did you immigrate like Grace?"

"I am from Philadelphia. That is where Benjamin and I met. After Harvard he arrived in Philadelphia to work as an attorney. We spent that first summer visiting every bookstore in the city. The Continental Congress was in session and we spent evenings discussing politics."

Olivia spent her life sewing and raising her six children. She did not have time to read or to discuss politics, to learn foreign languages or to paint master pieces. She did not hail from a wealthy, seafaring family who traveled the world.

"Running your own dress shop must be quite satisfying. You are wearing a lovely outfit. Clearly you are a talented seamstress," Grace complimented.

"I enjoy the sewing and dealing with my customers in town. I have brought a trunk filled with fabric. I know how busy all of you are with your responsibilities. I thought perhaps I could sew a few dresses for you in gratitude for your hospitality," she offered.

"Are all the fabric cotton?" Hannah asked.

"Oh yes. At one time we exported raw cotton to England who in turn exported cotton fabric back to us. Now with the cotton gin and new textile mills right here in our country, the price of fine cotton fabric has dropped substantially."

"Papa told me how Francis Cabot Lowell went to Bristol, England to visit the British textile mills. Apparently he memorized the workings of their power looms, returned to America and built his own power loom in Waltham.[1] They are now building a large textile mill in Saco[2] which will employ many people," Abigail explained.

"Of course the rise in demand for inexpensive cotton fabric increases the demand for the slaves to pick the cotton.

I would say there is a very high price to be paid for cotton," Hannah stated sternly.

Grace sensed Olivia's discomfort. "But Hannah what is the alternative? Mother Miller spent every free moment spinning and weaving linen and wool. Off course during the American Revolution many women had no choice but to clad their families in home spun linsey-woolsey. Today I appreciate the convenience of buying fabric."

"A convenient act does not equate a moral one," Hannah replied.

"Mama, you sound just like Papa," Abigail laughed.

"Perhaps your Papa sounds like me," Hannah responded.

The three boys noisily entered the house. "Eli is teaching me how to skip rocks," Asher said excitedly. "Tomorrow we will go to the hen house to get eggs and feed the sheep."

"After your lessons," Abigail reminded.

Ethan's first full day in Fryeburg was a pleasant one. Micah, Ethan and Olivia strolled through the village. "I remember helping father build this school," Ethan reminisced as they stopped in front of the original Fryeburg Academy. "It is sad to think of it sitting there vacant all these years."

"It is not vacant. The Unitarians hold their services here on Sundays," Micah explained.

"I never thought I would see the day that there would be Unitarians in Fryeburg."

"There was a revision of the church creed introducing new articles of faith. A number of dissenters left the Congregational church and established the Unitarian Society.[3] I want you to take a look at the new Academy building," Micah invited as they continued with their walk.

"The Oxford House looks busy," Ethan observed.

"Oh yes. Ever since New Hampshire built a turnpike through Crawford's Notch, many farmers loaded with hogs, cheese and butters plus merchants from Vermont and western New Hampshire have discovered that Fryeburg is about halfway to Portland for them. Many of them spend a night or two at the Oxford House."[4]

Ethan observed the new shops and businesses on their way to the new Academy building. "This school is rather impressive," he admired the large, two-story structure with the bell tower. "There are some fine new homes on Main Street," the brothers stopped in front of Dr. Barrow's home. "That is a well-built home," Ethan admired. "Fryeburg is growing prosperous."

Joshua spent the day at Benjamin's office while the judge was at court. Abigail proved to be a patient and skillful teacher as Asher was a bright and capable student. Abigail, Sarah and Grace made Olivia feel welcomed. Hannah and Kate stayed home to prepare a proper supper. Danny and Eli stopped by the farm after school to play with Asher for a few hours. After last night's misgivings, Ethan was hopeful that he made the right choice in bringing his wife and son here.

It was a beautiful evening as Ethan, Olivia and Asher strolled up the lane to Benjamin's house. Ethan brought his family to the elegant front door and knocked as a surprised Benjamin greeted them. "Ethan, you know you are welcome any time to just walk in the kitchen door."

"Benjamin, your home is beautiful," Olivia admired as she scanned the gracious foyer, the elegant staircase. Benjamin's magnificent law office had built-in book cases, Chippendale desk, upholstered furniture in the sitting area by the parlor stove and two oriental rugs."

"It should be beautiful, your husband designed and built it," Benjamin smiled.

"Did Sadie paint those pictures?" Olivia pointed to "The Portraits of Change."

"Sadie did all the paintings you see in this house. Now I want to show you your husband's handiwork in the dining room," Benjamin led his guests to the dining room where a black walnut table was set with blue and white china on an indigo table cloth surrounding by matching black walnut chairs upholstered in black leather. A side board stood between the two front windows. A black leather settee was placed against the interior wall.

Eli and Danny ran down the stairs into the dining room, "Nana says if we behave like gentlemen, we can play outside as soon as we are done eating and we do not have to sit there listening to the grownups' talking!" Eli with clean hands and face, brushed hair and a fresh shirt excitedly explained to Asher. Of course Asher never had a problem sitting still and politely listening to adult conversation.

Hannah, Abigail and Kate brought in platters of fried chicken, parsnips, asparagus and biscuits. Pitchers of cold water right from the well were placed on the table.

"Ethan, please tell us about your cabinet making shop," Benjamin invited.

"I have recently made some significant changes. We use water powered lathes and saws to produce large numbers of standardized chair parts. This greatly reduces the time it takes to fill an order as well as the price. I can sell chairs for $.30 to $.75 a piece."

"Would that not hurt your business to sell chairs so cheaply?" Jacob asked.

"On the contrary, it has increased my business. Families of modest means who could never afford my custom built furniture can now purchase a room full of matching chairs.[5] My sons can fill the orders without my help. That is why I am able to take this trip. Plus my wealthier clients will continue to order custom made pieces. We live in incredible times," he stated.

"What do you think of the upcoming presidential election?" Ethan asked his brother with a twinkle in his eye for he knew what his answer would be.

"Let us examine the evidence," Benjamin winked at Asher. "On the one hand we have John Quincy Adams, born in 1767 to educated and respectable parents, John and Abigail Adams in Braintree, Massachusetts. He is highly educated studying in private schools in Paris, Leiden and Amsterdam. He also accompanied his father on diplomatic missions in Europe during the American Revolution. He graduated from Harvard and served as Minister to the Netherlands and Prussia. He was the chief American peace commissioner in negotiations at Ghent ending the War of 1812 and is President Monroe's Secretary of State.[6]

On the other hand, we have four southerners: William H. Crawford of Georgia, John C. Calhoun of South Carolina, Henry Clay of Kentucky and Andrew Jackson from Tennessee. Out of these four southerners it appears that Andrew Jackson is the most popular.[7] He was also born in 1767 in a frontier settlement between North and South Carolina. His father, a Scotch Irish immigrant died a few days before he was born. He lost his mother and two older brothers during the Revolution. He did receive some formal education at local schools before studying with two members of the North Carolina Board. He migrated to Tennessee where he served as a member of Congress, a US Senator and the state militia. He was a successful major general in the War of 1812. The Battle of New Orleans made him a national hero. Did I mention he is a slave owner and lives on a plantation?[8]

The disparity between the two could not be clearer. Do you want an educated man experienced in international politics and a peace maker? Or do you want an uncouth, under educated soldier and slave owner?"

"I want John Quincy Adams for President!" Asher stated enthusiastically.

"I rest my case," Benjamin laughed.

"Four out of the five Presidents – George Washington, Thomas Jefferson, James Madison, and James Monroe were all southerners," Hannah continued.

"You make southerners sound like an evil to be avoided," Ethan responded. "You must understand that the majority of southerners do not own slaves at all. No one in Olivia's extended family has ever own a slave."

"Who are we to judge those who do have slaves? They are not breaking any laws," Olivia explained. "On the other hand, no one is forced to own slaves. It is a choice."

"What choice do the slaves have?" Hannah countered.

"There are plenty of northerners who have benefited from slavery. Look at Grace's family. The Peabodys made their living through shipbuilding. Some of those ships were used for the slave trade," Ethan illustrated. "Look at the textile mills springing up in northern towns. Where do you think the cotton which they spin into cloth comes from? Many factory owners are growing wealthy indirectly from slave labor."

"Slavery is like cancer. It must be eradicated before it kills this nation," Abigail countered.

There was a knock on the back door and Micah entered. "Benjamin, Mother wants to see you right away. She refuses to go to bed without speaking with you first."

"Micah, please join us for dessert," Hannah invited. "We are discussing the upcoming election."

"Mother, did you wish to speak to me?" Benjamin asked as he entered the drawing room where he found Sarah sitting in her chair with her beloved cat.

"Please have a seat," she motioned. "Is it true?" she asked sadly. "Is it true there are Unitarians meeting in the old Fryeburg Academy building?"

"Yes, Mam," he responded respectfully.

"The Trinity is the foundation of Christianity. To deny the Trinity is to negate Christianity itself. Man cannot fathom the mysteries of God. How can one God be in three Persons, Father, Son and Holy Spirit? Because man cannot exist in a trinity he insists that God is unable! Because man cannot comprehend an omniscient and omnipotent God, he insists that God must have limits. Man is created in God's image. Now they created a god who is in man's image.

Our Creator is to be worshipped and adored. They demand a god that can be understood. Jesus Christ was fully God and fully human. Man cannot be both so they insist Jesus cannot be as well. To deny the deity of Christ is to deny His atoning death, His glorious resurrection and His ascension. Yes, it is impossible for a man, yet it is possible for the Son of Man.

Heresy is like cancer; it must be removed before it spreads. Benjamin, you are a judge. You must stop them."

He gently took his mother's hands into his. "We may pray for them. We may debate them. We cannot stop them. This is America; we have freedom of religion. In Philadelphia, there were Quakers, Jews, Catholics, Anglicans, Presbyterians as well as Congregationalists who freely practiced their faith without molestation.

Mother, you and I are Bradfords, descendants of William Bradford who fled religious persecution in England and arrived in Plymouth on the Mayflower two hundred years ago. The Lord may call us to be persecuted, but never to be the persecutors."

"Micah, what do you think of this upcoming presidential election?" Ethan asked with a smile.

"I think there is no one better qualified to be our next President than John Quincy Adams," he answered.

"What about Andrew Jackson, the war hero, the man of the people?" he countered.

"Four of the past five Presidents have been slave owners from the South. This country needs to change direction."

"I do not believe it! You sound just like Benjamin!" Ethan's fondest memories of home were the political arguments between his two brothers.

"Sometimes our brother is right."

Life in Fryeburg changed more than Ethan originally surmised.

Life fell into a predictable rhythm. Every morning Asher eagerly awaited Abigail's arrival. After his lessons he would quietly retire to his bedroom to read and study. Later he would take a walk to the river, to secretly practice skipping stones and return to observe Sadie paint in the drawing room.

"What are you painting?" he asked.

"I am painting a picture of the field and the Saco River for you. I do not want you to forget Fryeburg when you return to Virginia," she replied.

After Asher's language lesson, Abigail spent the rest of the morning reading to her grandmother in the sunshine.

Grace was noticeably more relaxed with Abigail tending to Sarah and Olivia helping with the housework. She was now unencumbered in the mornings to work with Kate making butter and cheese. Kate and Rachel took over the delivery route. No one seemed to notice their visits to the Sanborn Farm in East Fryeburg or to her grandparents' home on Fish Street.

Grace and Olivia sewed in the dining room each afternoon while Sarah and Big Cat took a nap. "Williamsburg sounds like a lovely place. Winters here can be rather long and isolating."

"Summers there can be long and unbearable," she quipped as she enjoyed the breeze from the opened window. "I would love to have you come for a visit and meet the rest of the family."

"I would love to meet the family and visit your dress shop."

One afternoon Eli and Danny raced into the kitchen yelling, "Asher, we are here!"

The sound of footsteps running down the stairs was followed by "I fed the sheep by myself so we would have more time to play before supper." His mother looked at him sternly. "I mean my father and I fed the sheep together. But I got the eggs by myself."

"Boys, let your sister play with you," Kate admonished. Danny groaned as the three boys ran out with Rachel following.

"Asher never had friends before. He is so much younger than his brothers and being sickly and tutored at home he did not meet many children his age. We almost lost him last summer," Olivia confided with tears in her eyes.

"Perhaps he should visit every summer," Grace invited.

"Perhaps Kate could recommend a few remedies for his cough," Hannah suggested. "A mustard plaster can work wonders."

"I think I would begin with a mint and thyme chest rub," Kate explained. I will pick some from the garden this evening. All you need to do is to mix ½ cup mint and ½ cup thyme in two cups of sunflower oil. Heat it slowly without boiling. Massage into chest area at bed time.[9] A cup of hyssop tea three times a day may help as well." Hannah looked at her daughter-in-law with pride. "I will write down my recipes for you to take back to Virginia."

"How is Alden?" Ethan asked Micah as they unhitched the horses after a morning of plowing.

"The Erie Canal will be completed next year. With his wages and some inheritance from Grace's father he has purchased land along the shores of Lake Erie and plans to settle there and become a ship builder. He is also courting a young lady, the sister of his best friend. It was difficult to let him go, but Benjamin was wise in advising me to let Alden leave with my blessing. It is not easy for a father to let his only son go."

"Excuse me for interrupting but dinner is ready," Abigail invited.

Ethan noticed Joshua's twinkle in his eyes as he escorted her back to the kitchen and sat beside her at the table.

"Where is mother?" Ethan asked in concern.

"She is taking her nap a little earlier today," Grace explained trying to not reveal her alarm.

"I hope having us here is not tiring her out," Olivia apologized.

"On the contrary, I believe your visit has lifted her spirits," Grace assured. "I know it has lifted mine."

Sadie who did not follow the conversation blurted, "Uncle Ethan, I need some advice. I have several thousand dollars I made from the sales of my paintings. Papa says I should not deposit it in a bank. But what should I do? I cannot keep it hidden in my room forever."

"Your father is right. Firstly, Fryeburg does not have a bank. Secondly I would not deposit my life savings into a bank which may squander it in foolish investments. However, I do have the perfect solution," he smiled mysteriously.

XI

A New Venture

"You should buy hundreds of acres of forests."

"I am an artist. What am I going to do with trees?" Sadie asked perplexed.

"What can you do with trees? What can you not do with trees?" Ethan answered as everyone laughed at his enthusiasm.

"It takes over twenty cord of firewood to heat a house this size.[1] You can sell your hardwoods, maple, beech, birch and oak for fuel wood. Large white pines make excellent masts and spars for ship building. Hornbeam is ideal for ship trunnels."[2]

"No one in Fryeburg builds ships," Abigail interjected.

"The Saco River is 140 miles from the White Mountains in New Hampshire, through Fryeburg and empties into the Atlantic Ocean at Saco and Biddeford.[3] Shipyards up and down the coast buy their lumber from inland foresters who ship their logs down river."

Sadie looked skeptical.

"The town of Saco has seventeen saw mills just above the falls.[4] You would have a ready market," Micah agreed.

"Then you have your local markets. You can sell hemlock bark to the tannery in town. Your coarse woods like

157

hemlock and tamarack are strong and durable and valued in construction. Cedar is used for shingles.[5] People need lumber for casks, barrels and fences."[6]

"Who would I hire to do the work? This would take a large labor force," Sadie protested.

"That is the beauty of lumbering. The cutting of the trees must be done in the winter. Logs are dragged across the snow on bob sleds pulled by oxen to the river bank. When the river is running high in April with the snow melt and rain, it is time to drive the logs to the saw mills. The work needs to be done in the winter and early spring when all the farmers in Fryeburg have no farm work to do."

Jacob grew excited. "There will be no shortage of men looking for honest work in the winter. Plus most farmers would be glad to rent out their oxen for a few months. Do you understand what this would do for the local economy? By earning extra money in the winter and spring, people will have the means to build bigger barns or additions to their houses. This means they will need to buy lumber. They will want newer and bigger wagons and carriages. The local wagon makers will need to buy more lumber."

"They will have the money to buy more items from the local merchants instead of doing without or making do on their own," Abigail continued.

"People will make enough money to afford your paintings," Grace laughed.

"Who will supervise the workers? How will they know what to do?" Sadie protested.

"Your cousin Jacob and I will oversee the work," Micah offered. "We will start small the first year and gradually expand. That will give the two of us the opportunity to observe, select and train the hardest workers to become foremen in the future."

"Who will handle the money? Pay the workers? Sell the logs to the saw mills?"

"Your mother has a head for business. Abigail will assist her," Ethan suggested. "You pay each of them a salary to run the business while you earn the profits and paint. Uncle Benjamin and Joshua can draw up business contracts and oversee all the legal aspects."

"Think of the future generations of Millers. There is only one farm to hand down to one descendant. But there is enough land and work for all the grandchildren and great grandchildren," Ethan explained.

"If I can paint without interruptions and provide work for my family and neighbors, then we should investigate further," Sadie answered.

Three generations of Millers piled into two canoes at sunrise the following week. Micah, Ethan, Asher and Sadie led the way in the first canoe followed by Joshua, Jacob, Abigail, Eli and Danny. Ethan held a hand drawn map of land located below Swan Falls and before the Fryeburg Canal. Although the site was perfect, Ethan insisted that he scout the variety, quantity and quality of trees. "Pull up there," he pointed before he began paddling to the western shore.

"Papa, why are we stopping here?" Asher asked as he surveyed the gradual incline choked with undergrowth which led into the forest.

"This looks like poor land to me," Micah looked skeptical.

"It is poor farm land because it is rocky and uphill. But it is great timber land," Ethan explained. "The first step is to build a road to the river. See those tall, straight, white pines? If King George had seen those fifty years ago he would have reserved them as the King's pines to become masts for His Majesty's fleets. They will be the first to get chopped down to clear a path for the road. You will get good money for these and it will be easy to drag the logs down into the river."

"I understand," Jacob smiled. "All we might accomplish the first year is to build a network of roads into the property. Then we will need a small lumber camp, a stable for the oxen and maybe a shed to store hay and grain. The sale of these pines will cover our expenses and make a profit for next year. The following year, we begin logging in earnest, trimming and hauling the logs on ox drawn bobsleds to the river. When the ice is out, we drag the logs down the incline into the river."

"First we have to build the bob sleds," Micah reminded. "Only a half or a third of the logs will fit on the sleds. In addition to chopping off all of the branches, we have to hew off the bark on the portion of the log which will drag on the snow. This will greatly reduce friction and make it much easier for the teamsters to transport the logs."[7]

"I will build one or two samples of sleds for you to copy," Ethan offered. "Let us not count our chickens before they are hatched. First we need to scout out the trees."

Micah protectively helped Sadie up the hill and held unto her arm. "Papa, I am deaf. I am not blind," she complained.

However, Abigail did not protest when Joshua assisted her up the hill and continued to hold her arm. Asher soon grew tired and Ethan carried him on his back. Danny was tempted to whine that he was getting tired, but he wanted to be a big boy like Eli.

After a thirty minute hike Danny asked, "Are we lost? How will we find our way back?"

"Men never get lost. Remember that!" Jacob tousled his son's hair. "Remember that uphill is west to the mountains and downhill is east to the river."

A panting and perspiring Ethan stopped and put his son down in front of a large tree on top of the hill. "Do we have any volunteers to climb up and tell me what you see? This is a job for a younger man."

"I can climb the tree!" Danny eagerly volunteered.

"You are a little too young. I was thinking of your papa," Ethan laughed.

"Uncle Ethan, Papa is not young!" he argued.

"Just watch your old Papa!" Jacob grabbed his rope, threw it over a high branch, tied a secure knot and began propelling himself up the trunk until he reached the branches. From there he climbed the branches like a ladder up to dizzying heights. That morning Danny knew when he grew up he wanted to be a "tree man". Eli was convinced he would be a farmer with his two feet firmly planted on the ground.

"What do you see?" Ethan yelled up.

"Trees!" he joked. "I see a stand of birch. I see lots of pine trees or are they hemlock?"

"Hemlocks have smaller, darker green needles. It might be hard to tell from up there. Come on down. We will hike for another hour in a north westerly direction and then climb another tree. Four hours and three climbed trees later, Ethan had sketched a diagram with notations of the trees on their property west of the Saco River to the Fryeburg Canal.

"These woods are filled with white pines, the Prince of the Forest," Ethan grinned. "It is time to head back to the canoe."

That evening the entire family sat around the Liberty Table by the hearth. "If Uncle Ethan believes that this is a wise investment and if Uncle Benjamin can draw up the legal work, than I shall purchase this land," Sadie agreed.

"In fact, I am thinking of buying a small parcel of land by the Saco south of the canal from the Walkers. I think in the future it would be a great site for a saw mill," Benjamin informed. "Fryeburg is growing fast. The Academy will soon be expanding as well as the Oxford House. New families are streaming in. All will need lumber to build. When I am gone, my grandsons will be provided with a livelihood."

"Grandpa, where are you going?" Rachel asked innocently.

"Hush," her mother scolded.

"James would be proud of all of you," Sarah smiled at her family.

Word spread quickly throughout Fryeburg about the land purchase and soon men were arriving at River View Farm inquiring about future employment. The S.A. Miller Company would need barkers, to scrape the bark off the portion of the trees which would drag across the snow. They would need teamsters to oversee the care and work of the oxen, as well as cutters to chop the trees down. Micah recorded the names of men and the list of saws and tools they had to bring. Ethan asked them about their experiences in chopping trees and building. They were looking to hire a crew composed of mature men with practical experience as well as strong, young, daring men to meet the physical demands.

Grace was grateful for Olivia's help that summer. While Ethan was helping Micah, Jacob and Joshua with the crops and livestock and Abigail and Sadie were teaching school, Sarah was physically failing. Olivia competently assumed the housework so Grace with Hannah's help attended to Sarah. It now took two people to safely move Sarah from the bed to her chair, to bathe and to dress her. Ethan built a ramp for the back door so Sarah could be wheeled down in her chair and sit in the shade of a pine tree. She, with Big Cat on her lap, would watch Olivia sew and listen to the stories about her grandchildren in Virginia.

One evening Sarah was sitting outside with Hannah, Abigail and Joshua when she announced, "Joshua I have asked Olivia to make you a new suit."

"Mrs. Miller you have been more than generous to me these past five years. I cannot accept such a gift," he replied.

"Well, I want you to have a new suit for my funeral and other occasions. You cannot be wearing that old, brown suit of yours!" she replied.

"Yes, Mam. I mean no Mam," he politely responded before heading toward the barn.

Abigail ran after him. "There is nothing wrong with the way you dress," she defended. "Old Nana was just trying to ..."

"I understand. She was trying to give me a gift and not make me feel indebted to her. When she invited me to live here, she tried to make it sound as if I was doing her a favor by helping with the farm work."

"But you are doing us a favor. What would we do without you? You help Uncle Micah on the farm and you help Papa in the office. Who would I have to discuss politics and literature with at dinner? I cannot picture this family without you in it. Besides, I think you will look very handsome in a new suit."

"Who am I to argue?" he smiled.

One Saturday in late August an agent from Portland arrived at the farm to discuss with Ethan and Benjamin about finding buyers for the timbers. Ship builders and large saw mills along the coast often hired the services of agents to scout for quality timbers further inland. Ethan had been corresponding with one particular agent and invited him to evaluate the trees for himself. Benjamin was there to draw up any legal contracts.

"I have been a cabinet maker and carpenter for over thirty years and I have never seen such quality timber," Ethan enthused.

"I will be the judge of that," Mr. Sawyer responded as he jotted some notes into his journal. To the gentlemen's surprise, Sadie, attired in her gray silk dress, entered the drawing room.

"Good morning, Mr. Sawyer. I am Sarah Alden Miller, the sole proprietor of S.A. Miller's Enterprises. Before we do business I would like four references from previous landowners as well as a list of your clients who retain your services. I will not sell my timber to ship builders involved in the slave trade and I reserve the right of refusal."

"Look, Miss that is simply not done. I sell the timbers to the highest bidder. I am not in the business of screening potential buyers."

"I am not accustomed to negotiating. I will employ another agent to my liking. Also, I am perfectly content to simply hold onto my property for another decade. There are fools clear cutting thousands of acres. By then my timbers will be worth far more than they are today.

You may leave the names of your references and client list with my attorney. I do hope you have not wasted an arduous trip to Fryeburg. Good day, Mr. Sawyer."

"Well, since I am out here, I might as well take a look," Mr. Sawyer grumbled.

"You will not be sorry," Ethan promised as the two of them left the house and headed for the canoe waiting on the bank of the Saco River.

"Sadie, you are your mother's daughter!" Benjamin laughed.

"There is a time to be Micah Miller's daughter and there is a time to be Grace Peabody's daughter. Libby taught me that."

"My, the mornings grow chilly," Olivia observed.

"I do love September. Cool mornings are followed by warm afternoons. There is still daylight after supper," Grace explained.

Autumn held a new routine for the family. Abigail and Sadie completed the summer term at the academy. To Asher's dismay Eli and Danny returned to school. Abigail resumed tutoring Asher in Greek and Latin while Sadie began giving private art lessons in the drawing room three mornings a week. Sarah was content to spend those mornings watching Sadie and her students. Hannah cared for Rachel as Grace and Kate spent mornings making butter and cheese and delivering their wares. Asher helped the family pick apples in the afternoons and Ethan taught his son how to make cider using his old cider press.

"Olivia, you are a talented seamstress," Hannah complimented as the two women were picking apples. "Mr. Pierce's suit is as fine as any of Benjamin's. He has purchased some tailored in Boston and London. May I hire you to make dresses for Kate and Abigail? Both are hard-working, young women who deserve at least one elegant dress. With Abigail and Sadie available to watch Old Nana, we could spend afternoons at my home sewing."

"I would certainly enjoy getting better acquainted," Olivia smiled. Perhaps she misjudged this sister-in-law. Maybe Hannah was not cold and distant but merely shy.

"When the children were younger, Grace and I would spend hours together. But now Grace and Kate are so busy. It will be a pleasure to have some female companionship. I do want to hear more about your family. Six children and your own business! How do you do it?"

"Some days, not very well," Olivia laughed.

"Uncle Ethan, what are you making?" Eli and Danny could not contain their curiosity.

"This is called a toboggan. I thought since I am building some bobsleds to drag logs through the snow I may as well build something useful like a sled for my grand nephews."

"You are making something for us?" Danny asked in excitement.

"Of course I will need some help. Can you boys measure these four pieces of wood?" he handed his eager assistants a measuring stick. "Do you know what kind of wood this is?"

"It is oak," Danny answers with certainly. "Oak is very strong. Each board is ¼ inch thick."

"That is perfect. If a toboggan is too thick, it is difficult to curl the front end. If it is too thin, it will not be strong enough to withstand any crashes."

"They are four inches wide and ten feet long," Eli continued.

"Well done. Can you measure these seven boards for me?"

"They are all the same. They are one inch thick and one inch wide and sixteen inches long," Danny excitedly explained.

"Now if I put together these four boards and each one is four inches how wide will they be?"

"They will be sixteen inches just like these boards," Eli proudly answered.

"That is why carpenters and farmers need to learn their times tables," Ethan grinned.

"We are going to take those sixteen-inch boards and fasten them to these four to hold them together."

"I see how this will work." Danny preferred the smell of freshly cut wood to the odors of the barnyard.

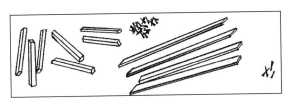

"A carpenter never nails anything without measuring first," Ethan warned. "Boys, after you measure twelve inches, draw a line with this pencil. Do that seven times.

Now it is time to nail on these cross-boards." With great concentrations the brothers held each board steady while Uncle Ethan nailed them into place.

"How do we get the front part to curve upward?" Danny asked.

"That is the fun part. Come back tomorrow after school," Ethan invited. "You boys should be heading home to get cleaned up for supper."

Fifteen minutes later the brothers reappeared with their grandfather. "Now this is a rare sight. The Honorable Benjamin Miller standing in my barn," Micah joked.

"We brought Grandpa to see our toboggan," Danny explained to Ethan who was sweeping the barn floor. "Grandpa, is this the most wonderful toboggan in the whole world?"

"Uncle Ethan is the best carpenter in America!" Eli added.

Benjamin and Micah looked at one another and smiled. "This is why Ethan was always the favorite," Micah laughed.

"Me? The favorite? Do not be ridiculous. Everyone knows that Micah was Father's favorite and Benjamin is Mother's favorite. I am no one's favorite," Ethan argued.

"Well then, you are my favorite brother," Benjamin consoled.

"No, Ethan is my favorite brother," Micah contradicted.

"I will have to be content with being the favorite brother," Ethan laughed.

The next day Eli and Danny ran all the way from school directly to the barn. "Uncle Ethan," they panted, "we got here as fast as we could."

"Perfect timing. I have completed building the forms. When I steam the wood, I will bend it around this shape. When the boards dry completely, I will pull out the forms and the front end of the toboggan will keep its shape. You boys may watch. This is not a job for beginners. It took me years to perfect this."

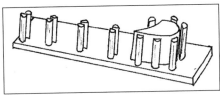

It was a cool October morning when Kate and Rachel took the wagon to make a delivery to the Wiley's farm. "Why do Eli and Danny go to school and I do not?" Rachel whined.

"You will go to school when you are seven," her mother explained.

"Why do girls go to school only in the summer at Fryeburg Academy and the boys go during the rest of the year?"

"That is the rule."

"I do not like that rule. Grandpa should change it. When I get big, I am going to go to the Academy with the boys. Danny says girls are not as smart as boys. I think Danny is stupid!"

"Rachel, do not call your brother stupid." As they turned down Fish Street Kate glimpsed Mr. Greene the slave catcher following her.

She fought the panic swelling inside as her thoughts were racing. Did he suspect her? Is he alone? Where is the other slave catcher? Why did she bring Rachel? What would happen if they got caught? What would her father-in-law tell her? This man had no right to stop her or to search her wagon. But what if he tried? She had her loaded rifle under the seat. Would she have to use it? They attacked Sadie five years ago when she was alone at Swan's Falls. She and Rachel were alone; the nearest farm was over a mile away.

As Mr. Greene headed towards them Rachel doubled over, held her side and began screaming in pain.

"Rachel! What is wrong?" Kate stopped the horses. Her daughter's screams grew louder.

Mr. Greene came trotting over. "What is wrong with that child?" he asked crossly.

"Please go back to the village and get Dr. Barrows. Tell him to meet us at my grandparents' house. Please get my husband at the farm."

The man did not respond.

"Go now!" she demanded over her daughter's screams. With that the wagon headed down the road as fast as the horses could run. Mr. Greene turned his horse around and galloped back to the village.

The Wileys came running out when they heard Rachel screaming as the horses pulled the wagon into the barn.

"What is wrong?" Mr. Wiley asked.

"Is the bad man gone?" Rachel asked as she sat up. "I did not want that bad man to hurt the black people hiding in the wagon."

Kate turned pale. "Rachel, what are you talking about?" She hoped her voice sounded calm.

"Mama, you do not have to worry. I have no intentions of telling my brothers. This will be our little secret. Do you think the black ladies would like some of my gingerbread?"

When Mr. Greene realized that he did not know where the doctor lived, he galloped directly to River View Farm. Before entering the barn he raised his hands as if to surrender. There he spied Ethan bent over finishing the toboggan and mistook him for Micah.

"Mr. Miller, I ain't after your horses. I am looking for your nephew – the one with the curly black hair. His wife sent me to fetch him and the doctor and send them to her grandparents. That little girl was awful sick, screaming her head off. I'd be obliged if you give them the message." With that he mounted his horse and trotted off.

Ethan broke out in a cold sweat. Mr. Greene had entered his cabinet making shop in Williamsburg on several occasions on business for his employer. Had the slave catcher recognized him?

"Jacob!" he yelled as he headed towards the fields. Jacob saddled his horse and galloped to his in-law's house. Ethan began packing. They would leave tomorrow at dawn to return to Virginia.

XII

The Election of 1824

The crops were in for the winter and the farm now felt empty. Micah and Jacob turned their attention to hiring men to build a road, a lumber camp and a stable before snowfall. Benjamin employed Joshua full time in his office as Fryeburg and the nation turned their attention to the upcoming election.

Benjamin and Micah rode together in Benjamin's carriage to join the other white, married, male property owners to vote at the meeting house in center Fryeburg. Simon Frye, nephew of Joseph Frye, handed each gentleman a ballot and checked his name written on a roster of Fryeburg voters. After voting, the brothers dropped their folded ballots into the slot of a square, wooden box under the watchful eye of John Hancock Frye.

Several men were outside espousing the virtues of Andrew Jackson, hoping to sway any undecided voters when Benjamin exited the meeting house. "May the best man win," the judge tipped his hat and smiled.

The next week, Benjamin's family and Joshua were seated for the evening meal. "I have learned that no one won the Presidential election."

171

"How is that possible?" Hannah asked.

"Apparently Andrew Jackson received 99 electoral votes, John Quincy Adams 84 votes, William Crawford 41 votes and Henry Clay 37. No candidate has won the required majority of electoral votes.[1]

"What will happen next?" Jacob asked.

"In accordance with Article II of the Constitution the House of Representatives will vote. Since by Article XII, only the top three vote-getters qualify under the circumstances, Henry Clay's name will be dropped from the list,"[2] Joshua explained.

"The House will choose from Adams, Jackson and Crawford," Benjamin continued. "I am grateful that the writers of the Constitution had the foresight to devise a solution to this situation.[3] Throughout history there are many examples of civil strife and wars to replace a leader. We are a country of laws and not of mob rule."

"Just look at the bloodshed in France. Between the French Revolution and the Napoleonic Wars there has been death and destruction all over Europe," Abigail agreed.

"We are a nation of laws," Benjamin repeated.

It was several days later when Hannah, Kate and Rachel entered the general store to purchase some sewing needles and thread.

"This is an outrage!" cried Mr. Abbott.

"I agree. The election was rigged," Mr. Bradley complained.

"John Adams is a monarchist and now his son has inherited the throne," Mr. Abbott continued. "How else can you explain that Andrew Jackson, who had more popular and electoral votes in the election, has now lost the election?"

"And the candidate with fewer popular and electoral votes has been elected to be the sixth President of the United States!" Mr. Walker concurred.

"Gentlemen, I believe it was Providence," Hannah smiled sweetly. "Three out of the four original candidates were pro-slavery southerners. Against all odds the one northerner who finds slavery to be an abomination, John Quincy Adams, becomes our next President. I call that the hand of God."

"Yes, Mam," Mr. Abbott doffed his hat respectfully.

There was one election that year which was irrefutable; the Maine State Legislature unanimously voted the Honorable Benjamin James Miller to be the United States Senator from Maine.

"Benjamin, what is wrong?" Hannah asked in concern when her husband returned early from court looking pale and shaken. "Are you ill?"

He sat in a chair by the cooking hearth and wordlessly handed her a letter.

"Senator! They voted you Senator! Benjamin, you could become another William Wilberforce! Instead of freeing one or two slaves at a time, you could write and pass an amendment to free all the slaves."

"I am not sure that I could leave Fryeburg," he said sadly.

"Mr. Pierce could run the law firm in your absence."

"I was thinking about leaving Mother."

"Our days in this life are numbered. Staying in Fryeburg will not lengthen her life. She may even pass away before the new session in Congress commences. She and your father would be so proud."

That evening the entire family gathered at the farm. Benjamin cleared his throat, "I have an announcement to make. The Maine state legislature has elected me to become a United States Senator."

Sarah clapped her hands in delight. "Benjamin, you could become the next William Wilberforce. Your father would be so proud! And Mrs. Merrill said you would never amount to anything." The family laughed at Sarah's indignation.

"Mother, do you think I should accept?"

"Mercy! Of course you should."

"Mr. Pierce, would you be willing to assume the responsibilities of the law firm in my absence?"

"Sir, I would be honored, providing that Abigail could assist me," he replied.

"That will not be possible. Abigail will of course be accompanying us to Washington."

"Grace depends on Abigail to help with me. I do not think I could bear for all three of you to leave," Sarah lamented.

"We also have an announcement to make," Grace beamed. "Alden is getting married next year to Gretchen DeJung. The Erie Canal will be completed. Alden is building a house in Buffalo that overlooks Lake Erie. The DeJung family is also moving to Buffalo where Pastor DeJung will begin a church."

"There will be Millers in Fryeburg, Boston, Williamsburg, Buffalo and Washington," Micah stated.

"But I am coming back," Benjamin reminded.

"You always do," Micah laughed.

Joshua gently knocked on Sarah's bedroom door. "Mrs. Miller, did you wish to speak to me?"

"I most certainly did." Sarah, who was in bed propped up with pillows, pointed to a nearby chair. He obediently sat down. "Now is the time to ask her."

"Ask who?"

"Abigail, of course."

"Ask her what?"

"To marry you of course!" she sighed in exasperation. "Why do you think I had that new suit made for you?"

"Mrs. Miller, you said it was for me to wear to your funeral."

"You may wear it to my funeral after your wedding. You need to ask her before they leave for Washington."

"How can I ask Senator Benjamin Miller for his daughter's hand in marriage? I have no property, no steady job and no prospects. What do I have to offer?"

"Perhaps that is my decision to make and not my father's," Abigail interrupted. "I have grown quite fond of your companionship, Joshua. I do not wish to leave for Washington, yet I will not be allowed to stay here alone."

"Perhaps it would be better for you to marry a younger man," he argued.

"All the younger men have married women who can cook and keep house like Kate," she replied resignedly. "Oh, I see," she blushed. "You do not wish to marry me and you are too kind to say so."

"Oh, but I do wish to marry you. The highlight of each day is sharing the evening meal with you, discussing politics, law and literature. You are not like other women."

"You mean that I cannot cook."

"No, I mean that you are interesting. You think for yourself. What other man could find a partner in the law firm and a partner in life? During these past five years I have watched you mature into a kind and thoughtful woman." He took her hands into his. "I know I have very little to offer you in the way of worldly goods. Abigail, will you marry me?"

The bans of marriage were read in church on Sunday morning. A quiet, family wedding was planned at the farm. It was decided that the newlyweds would live in Benjamin and Hannah's house during their absence.

One bright February morning Reverend and Mrs. Hurd arrived at the farm where they found Sarah dressed in her Sunday best, serenely sitting in her chair by the parlor stove. Kate was pleased to be the matron of honor and Jacob grinned as he served as best man. Eli and Danny were not happy about wearing their church clothes on a Saturday, whereas Rachel was delighted that her mother made her a new dress just for the occasion. Sadie, attired in one of her fancy Boston party dresses, studied the family gathering. Perhaps one day she would begin painting people. Benjamin had tears in his eyes as he escorted his daughter down the staircase and into the drawing room. Micah remembered the day he had given Libby away in marriage fifteen years ago. Hannah smiled in relief that Abigail finally found a good husband. Grace appeared distracted as she dwelled upon the dinner preparations. Joshua looked handsome in his new black suit. Abigail was radiant wearing her royal blue, silk dress designed and made by her Aunt Olivia. In a short and simple ceremony Joshua and Abigail were pronounced man and wife.

The entire family plus the Reverend and Mrs. Hurd gathered in the dining room where Hannah and Grace had prepared a ham dinner with baked acorn squash, boiled potatoes and apple sauce. Sarah listened to her family as they excitedly discussed the future. Hannah and Grace planned what Hannah should pack and take to Washington. Benjamin and Joshua discussed business. Sadie confided in Abigail that she might attempt to paint portraits of people.

Micah surprised everyone with an announcement. "I have made a decision which I know will please Mother and Father. Since my only son has decided to settle in Buffalo, I intend to leave the farm to Jacob and Kate in my will. In fact, you are welcome to move into the second floor. I need yearlong help with the farm, now that I have the additional responsibilities of the forestry business. Grace would appreciate Kate's help in managing the creamery and the house as she assumes her duties at S.A. Miller Enterprises. As soon as I find a good lawyer," he joked, "I will revise my will."

Joshua proposed a toast. "To the future."

Benjamin found Limbo sitting in his chair by the front window. "Come on in, Senator," he invited. "Look out this window and tell me what you see."

"I see Main Street, people, horses, wagons, the old Academy Building, the village school, the cemetery, houses, and stores. Is there something wrong with your eyes?" Benjamin was perplexed.

"None of this was here when I first came in the winter of 1762 with Nathaniel Merrill and John Stevens to pasture the cattle.[4] Look how this town has grown. At one time I knew everyone's name. Now I see mostly unfamiliar faces. Of course most people I knew now reside across the street," he nodded toward the cemetery.

"Speaking of the cemetery, I have come to say good bye and to let you know that I have purchased a grave site for you in case your time comes and I am not here. Jacob has the paper work."

"You can bury me with the white people? Is that allowed?"

"Tell people if they do not like it, they can write their senator," he joked.

"How can I tell people if I am already dead?"

"Limbo, you have been a good friend to me and to my family. Will you please try to visit my mother while I am away? I brought you some paper and ink for you to write to me."

"Benjamin, I have owned only one thing of any value in my life. I want you to have it." He shuffled across the room, opened a desk drawer and pulled out a leather bound journal. "Do you remember this?" he smiled.

"Of course I do. Hannah and I gave this to you thirty-two years ago."

"It took me years but I wrote my story and the stories of those who cannot write. Everyone should have a story, Benjamin. Everyone deserves to be remembered. Remember when you were a little boy and you taught me to read and write. That was a gift. Now be sure to write and tell me all about Washington. Good bye, Benjamin." Limbo stared out the front window to watch his old friend walk down the street.

That night Benjamin sat at his desk and opened up the journal.

I am called Limbo but that is not the name given to me back in Africa. My village was on the coast of Guinea. One of my jobs was feeding and caring for the silkworms. When I was an older boy but not a man I was kidnapped while I was out feeding the silkworms. I do not wish to remember the voyage across the big sea or my arrival to the American colonies.

Mr. McClellan of Gorham bought me. I used to drive cattle to the great Pigwacket meadows and winter them there. This was a long time ago before the town of Fryeburg stood. This was before the Millers came from Cambridge to start a farm by the Saco River. One day I ran away from my master and lived in Pigwacket. That was the name before they changed it to Fryeburg, named for General Joseph Frye.

Then I became a slave of Moses Ames. Later Mr. Samuel Osgood bought me for a yoke of oxen. Before he died he sold me to his son, James for five shillings. I guess I am getting old and not worth as much.[5]

Mr. Osgood was friends with Mr. Miller and I was allowed to spend some of my free time on their nearby farm. Their little daughter, Miss Abigail, taught me my Bible stories. It was a sad day when she died. Her brother, Mr. Benjamin, taught me to read and write. I practiced writing my letters on a slate. I can write as good as some white men in town. That boy was always in trouble for reading his books instead of doing his chores. I would eat meals with them at their table. It was a sad day when Mr. Benjamin left Fryeburg to go to school far away.

But one day he came back with a fine, young lady to marry. They had a trunk full of gifts from the big city they were living in. He gave me this here book. Who ever saw a book with no writing in it? He says I am supposed to write in it.

I don't have much to say. I get up in the morning like anyone else. I do my chores like anyone else. I chop wood like anyone else. I get water from the well like anyone else. I'm just like anyone else except I'm not free.

Mr. Benjamin asks me for help on a special project. Of course I say yes because I would do anything for Mr. Benjamin. I should say when Mr. Benjamin came back home he was the teacher of the new school in town. I know he's a good teacher because he taught Old Limbo to read and write. But now he had a whole school of boys to teach – and not just English. He taught them fancy languages and how our new government works. Then other people taught at the school and he spent his time in his big office with his books practicing law.

I forgot to say that he now lives in a big, white house that his brother Mr. Ethan built before he left to live in Virginia. You see when Mr. Ethan built this fancy house he built a secret tunnel that went right under the street to the house across the street. Mr. Ethan helps slaves escape from Virginia. They go from house to house until they come by following the river to the Miller's barn. One night I was hiding in their cellar when this poor boy is brought to the basement. Well I had my supplies packed and me and Thomas – that's the young one's name–are supposed to escape to Canada. Well, he and I went as far as...

Benjamin stopped reading and flipped through the pages of the journal. Limbo had listed the names of all the slaves plus information about their families, their owners and descriptions of the houses they hid in. It was Limbo's intent that if America ever freed the slaves, the journal might help reunite families. If the slaves were never freed, he did not want the names and stories of these people to be lost. They had a right to be remembered.

He understood the value of the book in his hands. It was a priceless history. He also knew if this journal ever fell into the wrong hands it would incriminate his family, his brother Ethan and many brave souls as well.

He carefully tore out the first two pages. With trembling hands he opened the door of the parlor stove and threw in the journal. He silently watched the flames consume an irreplaceable part of history.

Benjamin gently rapped on his mother's bedroom door. "Mother?" he whispered.

Her eyes slowly opened. "Are you leaving for Philadelphia?"

"No, Mother. Hannah and I are leaving for Washington," he sadly reminded.

"Your father would be so proud! You have the Lord's work to do and that work is in Washington."

"Yes, Mam."

"My work here is finished. I am ready to go home now. Do not cry Benjamin. You were always the sensitive one. Your father, sister and I will be waiting for you. I dearly miss them. My place is with them now. Your place is in Washington. Promise me you will write to your brothers."

For the third time in his life, Benjamin Miller left his home in Fryeburg to fulfill his destiny.

XIII

The Quaker Lady

Hannah was homesick. She missed everything about Fryeburg and despised everything about Washington. She missed her spacious home looking out on Main Street; she disliked the cramped, rented house on F Street. She knew she should be grateful for this little home because affordable, single family dwellings were few and far between.

For the past twenty-five years construction in this city focused on public buildings.[1] Then in August of 1814 during the War of 1812 the British invaded, burned and looted the unfinished Capitol Building on Jenkins Hill and the President's House on Pennsylvania Avenue.[2] Of course the city's efforts were focused on rebuilding these two structures. Workers finally had to paint the President's House white to conceal the scars left by smoke and fire.[3] In 1818 they connected the two newly repaired buildings of Congress. In 1820 they began constructing City Hall.[4]

There were shanties for the Irish laborers and dormitories for hired slaves working on the Capitol.[5] There were a significant number of mansions; many built as town houses by planters from nearby Maryland and Virginia giving the city a genteel, Southern flavor.[6] The majority of housing consisted of boarding houses, hotels and taverns for the senators, congressmen and others who viewed the city as a temporary home.[7] She would try to be thankful for this little house.

She missed the Maine summer breeze wafting through her open windows. Opening windows here allowed the dirt, noise and humidity to penetrate the house. The mud! Of course she was accustomed to mud season in Fryeburg but Pennsylvania Avenue was an impassable quagmire! She missed the sounds of nature – the singing birds, the chirping crickets and the peeping tree frogs. The city vibrated with the sounds of construction of horses and oxen pulling rattling wagons filled with tools and boisterous laborers.

How she missed Sarah, Grace, Kate and Abigail! She avoided the pretentious senators' wives with their teas, dinner parties and idle gossip. She missed the intimacy of her small Congregational Church and Pastor Hurd's simple preaching. Because there were few church buildings in 1801, President Thomas Jefferson decreed the Capitol Building hold nondenominational church services on Sunday mornings.[8] People appeared more concerned with what they were wearing or with whom they were sitting, than listening to the sermon. Last week she saw President John Quincy Adams and his wife Louisa sitting in the front row.[9]

However it was the sight of thousands of slaves which was most disconcerting to this sensitive woman. It appeared that half the population of the city was black; most of them were slaves. The availability of slave labor for the construction of new buildings was the result of the exhaustion of tobacco farming and its replacement of wheat farming. Because raising wheat was not as labor intensive, slave owners became interested in hiring out their surplus slaves who worked as waiters, domestic servants, artisans and laborers. There were numerous slave markets and auction houses operating in the city; one was located at Decatur House, in sight of the President's House.[10]

In contrast, where Hannah saw dirt and heard noise, Benjamin saw construction of democracy. Enthralled with his work, he would excitedly return home each evening and report the events of the day. Hannah tried to keep busy by reading or writing letters to home.

She reread a letter from Sadie.

Dear Aunt Hannah,

Rachel has proven to be a talented art student. She has an eye for color and pays attention to detail. I will not be surprised if we have another artist in the family.

I have begun painting portraits. Rachel is sitting for me. Mother made her a beautiful white dress with a lavender sash which looks lovely with her black curly hair. I know when you return from Washington she will be older and I wanted to capture her five-year old exuberance.

She is working on a painting of the lilac bushes in front of your house. When it is complete we will mail it to you.

Much love,
Sadie

How she missed the grandchildren! Although she dearly loved the boys, it was Rachel who stole her heart. Would she remember her Nana when they return in a few years?

When Benjamin arrived home that evening, Hannah greeted him with a smile, "You have a special delivery," she handed him an envelope addressed in Eli's childish scrawl *Senator Grandpa Benjamin Miller.*

He laughed as he sat down at the table and opened the letter.

Dear Grandpa,

Old Nana died in her bed. Big Cat is very upset and sits on her chair meowing. I went upstairs to cry so nobody would see me. Papa says Old Nana is in heaven with Old Grandpa but I wish she was still here with me. Aunt Grace says it is all right if Big Cat sleeps on my bed so he will not be lonely.

When are you and Nana coming home?

Your Grandson,

Elijah James Miller

He handed the letter to Hannah, put his head on his hands and tightly closed his eyes.

"There is another letter from Micah addressed to both of us."

Dear Benjamin and Hannah,

I know you will be upset when you hear of Mother's passing. She spent more time asleep in her bed than awake during the last few days of her life. I know that you would have wanted to be there with her like we were all with Father. However, even though we knew the end was coming, we were all surprised when it happened. She had a pleasant day before. She watched Sadie paint for a while and Abigail read some of Mrs. Adams' letters. She ate little at supper. She said she was very tired and Sadie and Grace put her to bed extra early. She died peacefully in her sleep sometime during the night. When Grace went to her room in the morning she found Mother had died.

Grace is simply inconsolable. In a moment of weakness I agreed to take Sadie and her to Virginia to visit Ethan and Olivia and then to Washington D.C. to visit with you. Alden will be getting married in Buffalo next spring and the Erie Canal is complete. From Washington we will sail to New York City and up the Hudson River to Albany and take the canal to Buffalo. What did I get myself into?

Benjamin, I know you, so please do not brood about this. She and Father will be waiting for us someday.

Your Brother,

Micah

The promise of a visit gave Hannah some hope. The next morning Hannah was meditating on the Bible verse "This is the day that the Lord hath made. Let us rejoice and be glad in it." She confessed her discontent and prayed for His will to be made manifest into her life. It was only eight o'clock that May morning and it was already hotter than Maine on an August afternoon. A gentle rapping on her back door caught her attention.

"May I help you?" she asked the child at her doorstep who was carrying a large wash tub and scrubbing board.

"Please, Mam, will you hire me to wash your clothes? I am much cheaper than all the other washer women."

Hannah stared at the filthy, black child dressed in rags. She was dirtier than the Millers' laundry!

"Please!" she whimpered as she closed her eyes and began to sway.

"When was the last time you have eaten?" Hannah asked as she put her arm around the child's slim shoulders and ushered her into the kitchen. "Do you have a name?" she asked as she handed her a slice of bread with butter and began to fry two eggs in a pan.

"Dora," she replied with her mouth full.

"Dora, who do you work for?" she asked tactfully for she had no intentions of paying some slave master for work she was perfectly capable of doing herself.

"I work for myself. I ain't no slave. We are a free family and we live by the Navy Yard."[11] My mama is having another baby soon and can't work. My older brothers and my papa work hard every day. Without Mama working, I need to work for myself."

"Did you carry that tub across town all by yourself?"

"I ain't no baby. I am almost ten years old and I'm a hard worker."

"You should be in school and not scrubbing other people's clothes."

"What school? There ain't no school."

"Help me fill that tub with water and…"

"I will scrub your clothes?"

"No, I will scrub you clean." Hannah scrubbed that child with a bar of soap and a clean rag and washed and rinsed her hair twice carefully checking for lice. "Now you put on this shift and take a rest on the sofa while I wash your dress."

Dora peacefully slept for three hours as her clean dress dried on the line. "Good afternoon," Hannah greeted. "Do you like stew?" she asked as she filled two bowls.

"Do you mean that bowl is just for me? I don't have to share it with nobody? Am I going to scrub your clothes after lunch?"

"No, you are going to mend your dress."

"I don't know nothing about sewing."

"Well, then it is time that a free girl like you learns. You know that I made all my children's clothes as well as my own. Sewing is an essential skill for a lady."

Hannah demonstrated how to thread a needle and how to make tiny, straight stitches. "Now, you finish. Free people learn how to care for themselves. Come back tomorrow and I will teach you how to make a shift and skirt."

"Can I wash your clothes tomorrow?"

"Yes, and while the clothes are drying on the line we will sew. There is no need for you to lug that tub home and back again. Leave it here. I will see you tomorrow."

"In time for breakfast?" she asked hopefully.

"Yes, in time for breakfast." Dora went skipping down the back steps.

The next morning two children appeared at the back door. "This is my brother, Lil' Henry and he needs a bath," Dora introduced the grinning eight-year-old.

"Good morning, Henry," she smiled. While you and Dora fetch some water from the well, I will fry some eggs. We will let the water warm up in the sun."

When the children entered the kitchen, the table was set, the teapot was ready and Hannah placed two fried eggs, bread and butter on each plate.

"Are you having company?" Henry asked.

"No silly, this is how free people eat," Dora explained. "Can we eat now?"

"First we give thanks, and then we eat," Hannah stated. "After breakfast I would like you, Henry, to sweep the front and back steps for me."

"'You want me to sweep the outside? That's plum crazy! What's Dora going to do?"

"It is not crazy. If the steps are swept then people will not track in dirt and dust to the inside. Dora and I will be having a sewing lesson." The night before Hannah had cut up an old white linen shift and a gray flannel petticoat to make a skirt and blouse for Dora.

Henry insisted that Hannah come inspect his sweeping. "I could not have done better myself. Here is some soap and cloths and now it is time for your bath. Put this shift on when you are done and come inside. Dora will wash your clothes and hang it on the line."

As Hannah and Dora sewed, Henry dusted the furniture and swept the kitchen. After lunch, Hannah placed two slates and some chalk on the table. "Do you know how to write your letters?" She wrote A B C D E F on each slate. "Please copy these while I sew. Do you know that each of these letters has a name and makes its own sound?" As Hannah sewed all afternoon, the children competed on who made the best letters.

"Dora, please try these on."

"I look like a little Quaker!" she whined.

"There are worse things you could look like. However, if you do not like these, I can give them to another little girl."

"Are you going to make me some new clothes too?" Henry asked.

"Perhaps if you help me with some chores and continue with your studies, I may make you some new clothes as well."

"Did Dora return today?" Benjamin asked as the two of them sat down for supper.

"Yes. I am teaching Dora and her younger brother Henry to read and to eat properly at the table."

Benjamin smiled at his wife's fastidious table manners. They both heard a quiet rapping at the back door. "I will ask your little friends to return tomorrow." However, he found not a little friend but a large, burly black man.

"Is this the Quaker lady's house?" he asked shyly.

"Yes it is. I am the Quaker lady's husband," Benjamin smiled. "Are you Dora and Henry's father?"

"Yes, sir. I hope they ain't making a nuisance of themselves."

"Please come in. My name is Benjamin Miller. Would you care to join us for supper? Hannah, we have company. Mr. I am sorry. I did not catch your name.

"Henry."

"Mr. Henry, Dora and Henry's father is here."

"I am pleased to meet you," Hannah greeted as she set an extra plate and silverware. "Your children are a delight and very bright I may add."

"My wife and I are most grateful that you are teaching them to read. Young ones can get themselves in a lot of trouble in a city like this. Money is hard to come by and I'm afraid I can't pay you right now for her new clothes and lessons, but I can trade some work in the yard for some lessons."

"Mr. Henry, your children work for their lessons and their meals. I find people appreciate things more when they work for them and not handed to them. Do you agree?"

"Yes, Mam."

"When I was a young girl growing up in Virginia I witnessed first-hand the ill effects of slavery. The white people frowned upon manual labor, believing that was the work for slaves. Therefore the master's daughters never learned to sew, cook or keep house. The master's sons never learned a trade or industry. The slaves, of course, had little personal interest in the life of the plantation and did a minimal of work. As a result, fences were out of repair, gates were hanging half off the hinges, doors creaked.[12]

Life in New England is much different. People are not afraid to work with their hands. Farmers plow, plant and harvest their own fields. Housewives sew their own clothes, cook their own meals and clean their own homes. People take pride in their work. I find it very disagreeable down here because it appears that no one knows how to work."

Mr. Henry listened politely as he self-consciously ate his meal. After he observed Benjamin cutting his chicken with a knife, he did likewise.

"I cannot remember slave families ever sitting down together at a table and sharing a meal. Children would eat a piece of bread here or a scrap of meat there. Sometimes part of the family would eat out of the skillet or pot because there were no plates or silverware.[13] Free people know how to keep house and sit down to eat a proper meal together. I am teaching Dora how to set the table and wash the dishes properly."

"Yes, Mam." He worked up his courage to ask the question for which he came. "Mam, do you think you could teach a grown man like me to read and write?"

"Mr. Henry, I do not think it would be proper to have my wife teaching men to read. That is why I will do it myself. I am a very good teacher. Thirty years ago I taught a class full of rambunctious farm boys. I think having one mature and serious student would be a joy. Shall we begin next Monday evening? Please stop by after work and join us for supper. That will save time," Benjamin invited.

By Friday Lil' Henry too looked like a little Quaker and both children had learned to write the letters of the alphabet.

"I will see you on Monday. I think we will plant a little garden."

"I'm ain't planting tobacco for some white lady!" Henry scowled.

"Hush!" Dora admonished.

"Planting tobacco would be silly. I thought we would plant some vegetables, herbs and flowers. My grandchildren are your age and they plant a small garden every summer. The fresh air, the exercise and the food will be good for you. Please bring your work clothes with you so you do not dirty your new clothes."

On Monday morning, seven children arrived to plant a garden. Hannah fried a dozen eggs and sliced a whole loaf of bread. That evening she wrote a letter to her sister-in-law Olivia.

Dear Olivia,

I find myself in need of a bolt of inexpensive muslin and gray or brown fabric, several spools of thread, sewing needles and lots of pins. There are few shops here in Washington that have reasonable prices .....

Monday evening Mr. Henry arrived and announced, "I've been practicing my letters with Dora and Lil' Henry."

Two weeks later green shoots were poking up through the soil and a wagon delivered the fabric and notions. A dozen excited children surrounded Hannah begging to be next to having new clothes. Hannah stayed up very late that night cutting out fabric. The rest of the week followed a predictable pattern: cooking, setting the table and washing dishes followed by a time of working in the garden, sewing, reading and writing.

When the children began to bicker as to who would get the next set of clothes, Hannah decided that they would start with the youngest child and continue by age to the oldest child. It was important for the older, stronger children to care for the younger ones. By the end of June each child had a bath and a new set of clothes.

One July afternoon Benjamin returned home early pulling a small wooden wagon. "I thought the children could use this to carry the vegetables home. Plus you could sell any surplus vegetables in the neighborhood."

Everyone excitedly talked about how they would spend their anticipated wealth. Benjamin interrupted, "May I suggest that any money you earn, you should purchase some chickens. You could eat breakfast at home with your families and sell any surplus eggs."

That summer, a troop of children "dressed like Quakers" pulled a wagon filled with flowers and vegetables up and down F Street peddling their wares door to door. The oldest children were responsible for the money.

"I think a few of you should sell bouquets of flowers on the Capitol steps at the end of the afternoon," Benjamin suggested. To their delight, they sold out of flowers on the first day. By the end of August they pooled their money to buy chickens and some lumber for a chicken coop. Mr. Henry with some other parents volunteered to build the coops. The children were excited to sell the surplus eggs to their neighbors.

One September evening Hannah turned to Benjamin, "I cannot imagine keeping those boys occupied all winter. I can teach the girls to cook and sew. Perhaps we can make a quilt and sell it. I cannot fit all twelve children in here at once to teach them reading and writing. I fear if the boys are bored they will get into trouble. How will I find a dozen pair of shoes for them?" she fretted.

"I am sure the Lord will find a way," he assured.

On Saturday afternoon a middle aged couple attired in simple garb knocked on their front door. "Senator and Mrs. Fox, how kind of you to drop by. This is my wife, Hannah. Hannah, this is Senator and Mrs. Fox from Pennsylvania. Please come in," Benjamin invited.

Once Hannah poured everyone a cup of tea and sat with them in the parlor Senator Fox began, "Your husband has told me all about the school you have opened for these children."

"School?"

"Mrs. Miller, you are feeding and teaching children to read and write and to master basic skills. I would call that a school," Mrs. Fox explained. "Some of us are anxious to assist you and to expand the school."

"I fear I do not know how I could possibly fit any more children in this house!"

"We would like to relocate to our meeting house. It would be a sin to let all that space go to waste during the week. There are several other Senator wives who feel called to teach these children."

"I discussed this with our elders back in Philadelphia and they are sending several carpenters to teach the boys the needed skills to get good jobs at the naval yard," Senator Fox continued.

Hannah grew excited. "Yes. The boys could do their carpentry in the mornings while the girls are reading and writing. After lunch the boys will have their academics while the girls are sewing. The boys can plant gardens in the spring and grow the school's food. The girls will make the school's uniforms and cook the meals. Perhaps the boys could build and sell some furniture and the girls could sew and make quilts and..."

Senator Fox laughed, "Your husband told me that you would make a fine headmistress! I believe he is right."

"Who me? A headmistress? I have never even attended a school," she argued.

"The children already know and love you. I cannot think of anyone better. I fear we can only offer you a modest salary."

For the first time in Hannah's life she would earn her own money.

"Hannah, you have been the headmaster's wife back in Fryeburg. Now I have the pleasure of being the headmistress's husband." Benjamin laughed.

"Mrs. Fox, may I suggest in the future we begin a night school for the adults who work during the day? I am sure that my student, Mr. Henry could recruit many students to the night school. Perhaps in lieu of tuition the men could perform some duties for the school.

When do we begin?" Hannah asked excitedly.

"Perhaps we could open a week from Monday. That will give us time to tell your students and to spread the word. We will need to build some long tables and benches for our students," Mrs. Fox took out a list. "Of course I will need to contact some of the other ladies who wish to teach. Perhaps Mrs. Miller, you could call a meeting with them next week. I think we should all become acquainted before commencing on this endeavor.

"May I bring the children to the meeting house on Monday so they will know the way? I would like to draw up a list of books and supplies that I would like to purchase."

"I know every book store in Philadelphia! I will purchase them," Benjamin volunteered.

When Hannah was a young child in Virginia, she never dreamt that she would be headmistress for children just like her!

XIV

Tea with the President

"May I escort you home, Headmistress?" Benjamin invited as he entered the school and stood by her desk one Friday afternoon.

"Is it four o'clock already!" she looked at the books and papers neatly organized into piles on her desk. "Well, Senator, I would be delighted. What time is everyone arriving? Should we stop by at the tavern? It is on our way."

The couple strolled arm in arm enjoying the spring sunshine knowing Fryeburg would still have snow on the ground in the beginning of April. "It will be good to see my brothers again," Benjamin broke the silence.

"It will be good to hear of all the news from home," Hannah added.

As they neared the tavern two carriages stopped by the front door. "It is them!" Benjamin hurried down the street pulling his wife along. "Can this be Micah Miller, the farmer from Fryeburg?" he teased his older brother who looked very handsome but uncomfortable in a brand new gray suit. He helped Grace out of the carriage.

"Oh Grace! I have truly missed you!" Hannah embraced her sister-in-law.

"I have so much to tell you! It feels like a hundred years since we have been together!" They laughed like two school girls.

"Ethan, the older you get the more you look like Micah," Benjamin slapped his younger brother on his back. "We have so looked forward to this visit. Where is Olivia?"

"She is in the next carriage with the ladies," he explained.

"Olivia, it is so good to see you again," Hannah greeted politely.

"Sadie! We have missed you! Did you enjoy meeting all your cousins?" Benjamin asked as two Negro ladies stepped down from the carriage. "Hello, I am Sadie's Uncle Benjamin."

"They are my slaves. I bought them for three paintings each," Sadie brusquely explained as the two women helped Sadie carry her luggage.

"Grace, you cannot be serious!" Hannah scolded.

"Let us get settled and freshened up and then we will meet for dinner," Grace evaded the issue as Micah picked up the luggage and headed up the stairs. "We will be at your house within the hour," she smiled.

Hannah fumed as she set the table for her guests. "Sadie has bought slaves! Benjamin, did you ever in your life!"

"Shhhh. They are here," he warned as he opened the front door. "Come on in. Everything is ready. Have a seat."

"Did you enjoy your visit to Boston?" Hannah asked coolly.

"Yes, it was wonderful to see Libby and the grand-children," Grace smiled. "We had the nicest time in Williamsburg as well."

"You should see Ethan's cabinet making shop! It is quite impressive. Not as impressive as his sons – five boys and they all look like Alden," he said enviously.

"You should come for a visit during your next break," Ethan invited.

"It is not that far and we would love to have you," Olivia offered.

"We will. I know Hannah is anxious to hear about her grandchildren," Benjamin changed the subject.

"Having Jacob, Kate and the family move in was the best decision we made. Sadie has moved into Old Nana's room and they have the entire second floor. Kate is a talented cook and homemaker relieving me of my many duties. This gives me time to devote to all the paper work for the lumber business. With them running the farm, we now have the freedom to travel and to visit our children and grandchildren."

"How is Abigail?" Hannah asked anxiously.

"I have never seen a couple more excited to have a baby. I understand how it feels to be miles away when your daughter has her first child. Do not worry about anything. She is in excellent health and Kate and Mrs. Wiley will attend the birth."

"This is from Rachel. She thought it would make your house pretty," Sadie handed her a square, flat package wrapped in muslin.

"Thank you, Sadie," Hannah politely but stiffly responded as she opened the gift. "It is beautiful!" she whispered as tears filled her eyes. The canvas was splashed in a riot of greens and purples. "They are my lilac bushes. Look how colorful. You are a good teacher," she complimented.

"How are the boys?" Benjamin asked.

"Eli and Danny are doing well in school and spend every afternoon helping us on the farm. Joshua is busy at the office. I understand he has several new clients now. Reverend and Mrs. Hurd send their greetings," Micah reported.

"Olivia, did you make Micah's suit?" Hannah asked.

"I am afraid we kept Olivia very busy. In addition to the suit, she made several dresses for me for the wedding and visiting. I must tell you I wish we had someone like Olivia in Fryeburg," Grace lamented.

"I also brought some old fabric for you. I thought your girls could make a quilt," Olivia offered. "I do want to hear about your school."

"Perhaps tomorrow we will give you a tour of the school and the Capitol. We could also take a walk down Pennsylvania Avenue to look at the President's House," Benjamin suggested.

"How is old John Quincy?" Ethan teased. "When Benjamin was a boy he was so jealous of him because he studied in Paris and traveled Europe," he explained to his wife.

"I have only seen him from afar at church. He is a serious minded fellow and does not socialize easily. That is enough about John Quincy Adams. We want to hear about life in Williamsburg. How is Asher?"

"He is diligently studying and talks about attending Fryeburg Academy in two years."

They talked well into the evening and made plans for the next day.

Although it was Saturday, the school was bustling with activity. "Welcome to the Freemen's School," Hannah proudly invited. "The men and boys are building a barn," she pointed to the timbers lying on the ground. "We hope to have a barn raising next month and have the barn finished for September. This will house the wood working shop. Wagons are in great demand here in the city. We hope to train the boys in wagon building and wheel making. We can sell the wagons to help support the school and provide our graduates with the skills to have their own business.

This plot here will be our garden to provide food for the students. They will have the opportunity to sell any surplus to the community. The way these boys eat, I truly doubt there will be much left over to sell," Hannah laughed.

They were enthusiastically greeted by Mrs. Fox and several girls as they entered the meeting house. "Mrs. Miller, is this your family? Did you show them our quilt? Did you show them our books? Did you show them..."

"This is Dora, my first pupil," Hannah wrapped her arm affectionately around the exuberant eleven-year old, "and our best seamstress. These two gentlemen are Senator Miller's brothers. This is Mrs. Miller from Fryeburg and Mrs. Miller from Williamsburg."

"I have a crate of discarded fabric to donate to the school," Olivia explained to Mrs. Fox. "They may be appropriate to make several quilts."

Dora clapped her hands in glee. "Can I see them now? Can I get them? I could load our wagon and bring them to the school. Can I ..."

"Dora, I will make arrangements for the fabric to be delivered. We do not wish for them to get dirty and dusty by a ride in an open wagon," Hannah explained firmly.

"Also I wish to discuss the possibility of taking in an apprentice. I am looking for a twelve or thirteen-year-old girl who has demonstrated an interest and ability in dress making. She will live with us and work in my shop until the age of twenty-one. By that time she will have acquired the necessary skills and experience to work for another seam-stress or open a shop herself. I would offer free room and board and a modest stipend."

"Olivia, I do not know what to say. That is truly generous of you." Hannah had to confess that she was wrong to quickly assume that all southerners were slave owners or callous by standers. "I think I have just the young lady in mind."

"I would also like to hire an apprentice for my cabinet making shop," Ethan continued. "With the boys getting married and moving out, we have plenty of room at home. I always have more work than I can handle. Besides freedom does not mean anything if you are unable to provide for yourself and family."

"This is truly providential," Hannah had tears in her eyes.

"The other ladies will be thrilled!" Mrs. Fox continued. "We have ten other wives of senators and congressmen from all over the country who are assisting us in our endeavors. We plan to begin a night school for those who work during the day. We will have a different staff of instructors for the night school. Mrs. Miller has her hands full with the forty-five day students."

"I have made many new friends this year. There are many women like me who are new in town and desperately miss their families back home. The school has given all of us a purpose in life during our stay in Washington." Hannah had to confess that she was wrong to quickly assume that all the other Washington wives were petty socialites.

Grace looked at her quiet, modest sister-in-law with a newfound admiration.

Sunday morning Hannah and Benjamin arrived at the tavern where they found everyone but Sadie waiting for them. "Hannah, would you be so kind as to go to Sadie's room and tell her we are ready. I believe she did not hear me when I knocked on her door," Grace asked sweetly.

Hannah smiled on the outside but protested on the inside. Because there was no answer when she knocked on the door, she entered without an invitation. There she found her niece dressed in her "Boston party dress" sitting on the bed.

"Aunt Hannah, please do not be upset with me," Sadie began.

"You are a young woman capable of making your own decisions. You need not ask for my approval," she answered curtly.

"Those two ladies are Millie and Ella, George's mother and sister. It was the only way we could think of getting them safely to freedom."

"To freedom?"

"Of course. They will be escorting me to Buffalo where I plan to stay for a year. Alden tells me there is a waterfall out there that I must paint. During my stay we will track down George and make arrangements for the family to be reunited in Canada. Buying them was the only way to get them safely out of town. Please think of Uncle Ethan. How would it look if two slaves are missing after his Yankee family left town?"

"Sadie, please forgive me. I am truly ashamed. I was too quick to jump to conclusions."

"Aunt Olivia is very nice. You should try to like her," she chastised.

"Once again, you are correct. I will take your advice," she humbly replied. "They are waiting for us and we do not wish to be late."

The family walked down F Street and turned left onto Delaware Avenue which lead directly to the Capitol building.[1]

Hundreds of people were walking or riding to the Capitol. "Since Thomas Jefferson's presidency, religious services have been held in the Capitol's Hall of the House of Representatives. These interdenominational services are overseen by the chaplains and preached by the chaplains on a rotating basis and by visiting clergy.[2] In January Catholic Bishop John England of South Carolina preached here."[3] Benjamin explained as they climbed the steps.

"All these people are coming to church?" Micah asked.

"In addition to the service we will be attending, there are four other churches, Capitol Hill Presbyterian, Unitarian Church of Washington, First Congregational Church and First Presbyterian Church, also meet in this building. There are also church services in the Treasury Building and the Supreme Court Building,"[4] Hannah continued.

They attempted to sit as far up front as possible so Sadie could read the preacher's lips. About as many people acknowledged Hannah as Headmistress, as Senator Miller from Maine. Ethan discreetly studied the architecture of the building; Grace and Olivia studied the ladies' dresses. Micah who had never seen so many people at one time nervously pulled on his collar. Sadie studied the colors and the sunlight pouring through the windows. Mercifully, just as the hall was growing uncomfortably warm, the service ended. Micah gasped a breath of fresh air as they stepped outside.

"Senator Miller? Senator Benjamin Miller from Maine?" a dignified voice from behind asked. Benjamin turned around quickly.

"Mr. President! It is an honor to make your acquaintance, sir."

"This must be your lovely wife, the headmistress at the Freemen's School."

"Yes, sir. I am so pleased that you have heard of our school," Hannah replied with her new found confidence.

"Is your family visiting with you?"

"Mr. President, may I introduce you to my older brother Micah Miller from Fryeburg and his wife, Grace."

"I have had the honor of knowing the Amazing Grace Peabody since my boyhood. I am delighted to have the opportunity to meet again."

"Mr. President," she charmingly smiled and offered her hand. "This is our younger daughter, Sadie."

"Yes, Sadie the famous artist." Turning to Ethan the President continued, "You must be the younger brother, the furniture maker in Williamsburg."

"Ethan Miller, Sir. This is my wife, Olivia."

"There you are my dear," President Adams turned to his wife, Louisa. "Mother was dear friends with the Miller family. How long is your visit?" he asked Grace.

"I am afraid we must all be leaving tomorrow."

"Then please come for tea at four o'clock this afternoon. We have decades to discuss." The couple entered their carriage and headed down Pennsylvania Avenue.

"I must tell you I never expected this," Grace gasped. "I did not expect that he would look so old." Micah secretly smiled at that comment.

The ladies were too nervous to eat lunch. Benjamin suggested that they take F Street and walk to the President's House. The ladies declined stating they would arrive hot and dusty. They compromised by hiring two carriages to tea and walking home by Pennsylvania Avenue to see the sights.

"Here we are," the driver stopped in front of a large white mansion. Micah did not relish relinquishing some of his hard earned cash for a needless ride. However, one thankful smile from Grace made it worthwhile.

"The brick building with the white columns to the left is the Treasury and State Department Building. The matching brick building to the right is the Departments of War and Navy,"[5] Benjamin pointed out as he opened the wrought iron gate and led the family up the semicircular path to the front door.

A Negro servant answered the door and led them to the green room where they found John Quincy and Louisa Adams seated.

"Welcome," the President formally invited them to take a seat.

"There have been many changes since the last time I was here," Ethan observed.

"I did not realize that you have been here before."

"It was December of 1800 and I was on my way to Williamsburg. Of course Mother insisted that I drop by to visit your mother. Only six rooms had been finished – or should I say nearly finished. She was drying her laundry in the unfinished audience room.[6] The portico had not yet been

203

built. This was before the War of 1812, and the house was not as white. It was more of a gray. She made me feel right at home as we had tea and talked about our families. I met your father briefly when I delivered a gift."

"The desk," John Quincy replied knowingly. "You would be pleased to hear that my father still uses that desk in Quincy."

"How is your father?" Grace inquired.

"His eye sight grows dim and his limbs are stiff and feeble. He is bowed with age and can scarcely walk across a room without assistance.[7] He is most eagerly anticipating the fiftieth anniversary of the signing of the Declaration of Independence this July 4th. Do you still have the Liberty Table?"

"Why, yes we do," Benjamin replied in surprise.

"Louisa, did I ever tell you the story of James Miller and the Liberty Table? As you know King George had his surveyors mark the tallest and straightest white pines in the forests reserving them to be used as masts for His Majesty's ships. Their father, James, had one in his woodlot in Fryeburg. When news of the signing of the Declaration of Independence reached Fryeburg, their family–with half of the village–chopped down that King Pine. Mrs. Miller announced, 'Some men declare their independence with a stroke of a pen; others by a swing of the axe.' They used that lumber to build a great trestle table and benches for their home. Mother read and reread that letter to us a hundred times. How is your dear mother?"

"She passed away last year," Micah replied.

John Quincy shook his head. "I am so very sorry for your loss. The arrival of one of your mother's letters was cause for a celebration when I was a child. How I envied you boys!"

"You envied us, sir?" Benjamin asked in surprise.

"As you know, my father was gone during most of my younger boyhood. When I left for Europe with my father,

I left my mother behind. I envied that you grew up under the love and protection of both your parents. Of course I envied the freedom and adventures you had. Your parents taught you at home – no private boarding schools for you. You played with the Indian children, you hiked the woods."

"Micah and I hiked the woods. Benjamin stayed in the house and read books," Ethan corrected. Benjamin glared at his younger brother.

"Senator, I fear you and I have much in common," the President laughed good-naturedly. "Do you enjoy politics?"

"I naively arrived in Washington hoping to become the next William Wilberforce. I am dismayed by the power and influence wielded by the southern senators," Benjamin confessed.

"I fear this nation is becoming two nations."

"Do you really swim in the Potomac River every morning?" Sadie innocently blurted.

"Indeed I do. Before sunrise during the hot months I take an invigorating swim.[8] You have the Saco River to enjoy and I have the Potomac.

Senator, we must meet again. Grace, it has been a pleasure to see you again and to meet your husband." The President arose indicating that their brief visit had come to a close. "I wish you all a safe journey home."

The same servant ushered them out the door. The Millers stood in Pennsylvania Avenue staring at the white mansion.

"We just had tea with the President of the United States," Olivia stated in disbelief.

"We have Grace to thank for that," Hannah teased. The ladies excitedly talked as they walked ahead down the avenue.

"We live in extraordinary times," Benjamin began. "We were born British subjects and we are now American citizens. We have witnessed the birth of a new nation, the inventions of oil lamps and parlor stoves. We can now travel by steam or sailboat on oceans, rivers and canals. We have watched Fryeburg, our children and grandchildren grow. We have migrated from Fryeburg to Boston, to Williamsburg, to Washington and Buffalo. I wonder where our grandchildren and great grandchildren will travel."

The brothers silently walked on realizing that this would be the last time the three of them would be together. Tomorrow the cabinet maker would return to his shop in Virginia, the farmer would travel the Erie Canal to visit his son before returning to his farm and the senator would remain in Washington for two terms.

"I wonder what life will be like twenty years from now." Ethan asked.

Fryeburg Landmarks

Fryeburg Academy founded in 1792 it is one of the oldest private schools in the United States serving a widely diverse population of local day students and boarding students from around the world. www.fryeburgacademy.edu

The Judah Dana House was built in 1816 on the corner of River Street and Main Street by Judah Dana, the first attorney in Fryeburg and Oxford County. Senator Dana's career was the inspiration for Benjamin Miller's life. In 1956 this historic home was torn down to build the Fryeburg Post office. Several local children entered the granite-lined tunnel which went under Main Street to the former Eckley Stern's residence across the street. According to oral tradition this home was part of the Underground Railroad.

The Oxford House has been part of Fryeburg's history since James and Abigail Osgood rented out rooms in their Main Street home. In the late 1800's and early 1900's The Oxford House Hotel was a grand 100 room hotel before it burned to the ground in 1906. Today the Oxford House Inn is a country inn and gourmet restaurant built on a portion of the site of the hotel. www.theoxfordhouse.com

Weston's Farm was established in 1799 and is a seventh-generation family farm located on 200 acres by the Saco River. www.westonsfarm.org.

The Benjamin Wiley House incorporates in its ell one of the oldest standing buildings in Fryeburg, a two-story wood frame structure built in 1772. According to oral tradition this house was part of the Underground Railroad and has a hidden room. The current owners provided me with the location and dimensions of this room.

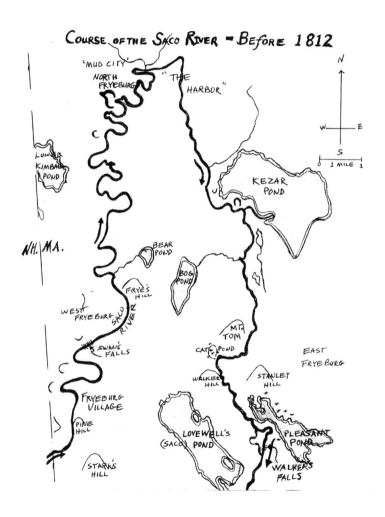

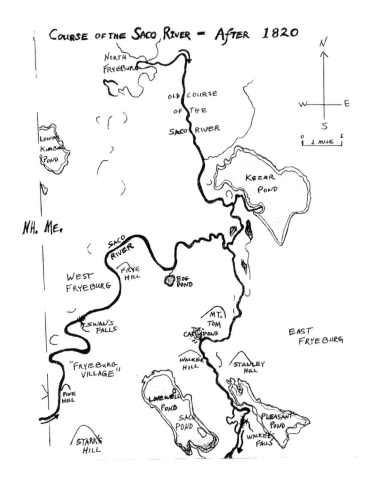

Discussion Questions

1. What was the impact of the Napoleonic Wars on the American economy?
2. What caused the Panic of 1819? What role did the state banks play in the Panic? Compare and contrast the causes of the Panic of 1819 to our recent recession.
3. What groups of people were for the independence of Maine? Who opposed independence? Why?
4. Described the Missouri Compromise of 1820. Who crafted it? What was the result?
5. Why was the Erie Canal an incredible engineering feat? Where was it located? What bodies of water did it connect? How do locks work? What impact did it have on the local economies? What impact did it have on the national economy? Who worked on the Canal?
6. What was the significance of Washington Irving? What did he write? What impact did he have on American literature?
7. What was the significance of Noah Webster? What did her write? What impact did he have on American education and language?
8. Describe the Washington, D.C. of 1825? How did the War of 1812 impact its history? What buildings held

church services? Why? What U.S. President initiated this practice?

End Notes

Chapter I The Funeral

1. John S. Barrows, <u>Fryeburg Maine: An Historical Sketch </u>(Fryeburg, ME Pequawket Press, 1938), pg. 89. Reverend Hurd was pastor from 1823-1855.
2. Barrows, pg. 174
3. Barrows, pg. 61
4. King James Version John 14:6

Chapter IV Graceless

1. www.encyclopedia.com/topic/Panic_of_1819.aspx.
2. Ibid
3. Ibid
4. http://en.wikipedia.org/wikicoinage_Act_of_1792.
5. www.thehistorybox.com.
6. Thomas Tusser, <u>Five Hundred Points of Good Husbandry</u> 1573.
7. Barrows, pg. 256
8. http://www.merriam-webster.com/info/noah.htm
9. Washington Irving, <u>Washington Irving's Sketchbook</u> (New York. Avenel Books, 1985) pg. 11. Foreword by Philip McFarland.
10. Mark Zanger, <u>The American History Cookbook</u> (Westport, CT. Greenwood Press. 2003) pg. 67.

11. James Bowden, <u>Maine in the Early Republic: From Revolution to Statehood </u>(University Press of New England. 1988.) pg. 9.
12. Bowden, pg. 1.
13. Bowden, pg. 84
14. Barrows, pg. 157
15. Barrows, pg. 160-161.
16. David McCullough, <u>John Adams</u> (NY. Simon & Schuster. 2001) pg. 104
17 Henry Graf, <u>The Presidents: A History Reference.</u> (NY. Simon & Schuster. 1997) pg. 92.
18. Ronald Banks <u>Maine Becomes a State</u> (Somersworth, NH. NH Publishing Company. 1973) pg. 149.
19. Bowden, pg. 15.
20. Banks, pg. 149
21. Barrows, pg. 196

Chapter V The Suitor and the Scholars

1. Jack Larkin, <u>The Reshaping of Everyday Life: 1790-1840</u> (Harper Collins) pg. 144
2. http://en.wikipedia.org/wiki/William_Wilberforce.
3. Bill Laws, <u>Fifty Plants that Changed History </u>(Allen & Unwin 2011) pg. 168.
4. Monica Brandies, <u>Ortho's Guide to Herbs</u> (San Ramon, CA. Solaris Group 1997)
5. Ibid.

Chapter VI The Judge's Verdict

1. Martha Kendall, <u>The Erie Canal</u> (Washington, D.C. National Geographic Society 2008) pg. 30.
2. www.eriecanal.org
3. Kendall, pg. 7
4. Kendall, pg. 8
5. Kendall, pg. 52
6. Kendall, pg. 54

7. www.eriecanal.org
8. Kendall, pg. 12
9. Barrows, pg. 135
10. Barrows, pg. 259
11. Barrows, pg. 136
12. Kendall, pg. 31
13. Kendall, pg. 33
14. Kendall, pg. 36
15. Kendall, pg. 38
16. Kendall, pg. 39
17. Kendall, pg. 46
18. Kendall, pg. 47
19. Kendall, pg. 54
20. Kendall, pg. 55
21. Kendall, pg. 57
22. Kendall, pg. 58

Chapter VII Abigail at the Farm

1. Washington Irving's Sketchbook was published in 1820.
2. This event happened in 1826. http://en.wikipedia.org/wiki/Crawford_Notch.
3. McCullough, pg. 467.
4. McCullough, pg. 480.
5. McCullough, pg. 481
6. Ibid
7. Ibid
8. McCullough, pg. 487
9. McCullough, pg. 490
10. McCullough, pg. 491
11. Ibid
12. Ibid
13. McCullough, pg. 552-553
14. McCullough, pg. 553
15. McCullough, pg. 551
16. Ibid

17. McCullough, pg. 553

Chapter VIII Merry Christmas
1. www.whychristmas.com
2. Ibid
3. Friedman, pg. 98
4. Friedman, pg. 120
5. Excerpts taken from "The Incarnation and the Birth of Christ" sermon # 57 preached by C.H. Spurgeon on 12/23/1855 in Southwark, England. http://www. spurgeon.org.sermons/0057.htm.
6. www.parkstreet.org/
7. www.whychristmas.com

Chapter IX Parlor Stoves
1. Larkin, pg. 136
2. Larkin, pg. 141
3. King James Version Isaiah 46:4, Psalms 37:25
4. Kendall, pg. 61
5. Ibid
6. Kendall, pg. 63
7. Banks, pg. 184
8. Ibid
9. Ibid
10. Banks, pg. 189
11. Ibid
12. Banks, pg. 190
13. McCullough, pg. 601-602
14. Shepherd, pg. 236-237
15. Cynthia Black, <u>Natural & Herbal Family Remedies</u> (North Adams, MA, Storey Publishing, 1997) pg. 11.
16. Ibid

Chapter X The Visit
1. http://en.wikipedia.org/wiki/Francis_Cabot_Lowell

2. http://www.mainememory/.net/sitebuilder/site/760/page1169/display
3. Barrows, pg. 90
4. Hattie A. Pike, The Lewiston Journal, The History of the Oxford House
5. Larkin, pg. 139
6. Graf, pg. 92
7. Graf, pg. 94
8. Graf pg. 106
9. Black, pg. 11

Chapter XI New Ventures
1. Bowden, pg. 2
2. Bowden, pg. 22.
3. Smith pg. 13
4. pg. 24
5. Ibid
6. Bowden, pg. 83
7. Ibid

Chapter XII The Election of 1824
1. Graf, pg. 94
2. Ibid
3. Ibid
4. Barrows, pg. 242
5. Ibid

Chapter XIII The Quaker Lady
1. Joseph Passoneau, <u>Washington Through Two Centuries</u>, (NY Monacelli Press, Inc. 2004) pg. 39
2. Passoneau, pg. 41
3. Ibid
4. Passoneau, pg. 44
5. Frederick Guthein, <u>Worthy of the Nation</u> (Baltimore, John Hopkins University Press 2006) pg. 39

6. Ibid
7. Ibid
8. www.wallbuilders.com
9. www.loc.gov/exhibits/religion/re106-2http
10. Ibid
11. Guthein, pg. 51
12. Booker T. Washington <u>Up from Slavery</u> (Williamstown, MA Corner House Publishers 1971) pg. 8
13. Washington, pg. 9

Chapter XIV Tea with the President
1. Passoneau, map on pg. 33
2. www.wallbuilders.com
3. www.loc.gov/exhibits/religion/re106-2http
4. Ibid
5. Passoneau, pg. 39
6. Shepherd, pg. 210-211
7. Shepherd, pg. 272
8. Shepherd, pg. 302.

Bibliography

Books:

Banks, Ronald F. Maine Becomes a State. Somersworth, NH.__N.H. Publishing Company/Maine Historical Society. 1973

Barrows, John Stuart. Fryeburg Maine: An Historical Sketch. Fryeburg, ME. Pequawket Press. 1938

Bennett, Randall H. Oxford County, Maine A Guide to Its Historic Architecture. Bethel, ME. Oxford County Historic Resource Survey. 1984

Black, Cynthia. Natural & Herbal Family Remedies. North Adams, MA. Storey Publishing. 1997.

Bowden, James S. Maine in the Early Republic: From Revolution to Statehood. University Press of New England 1988

Brandies, Monica. Ortho's Guide to Herbs. Solaris Group. San Ramon CA. 1997

Friedman, Debra and Larkin, Jack, editors. Old Sturbridge Village Cookbook. Guilford, CT. Three Forks, 2009

Graf, Henry F. editor The Presidents: A Reference History. New York. Simon & Schuster Macmillan. 1997

Guthein, Frederick and Lee, Antoinette. Worthy of the Nation. Baltimore. John Hopkins University Press. 2006.

Irving, Washington. The Sketch Book. New York. Avenel Books. 1985

Kendall, Martha. The Erie Canal. Washington, D.C. National Geographic Society. 2008

Larkin, Jack. The Reshaping of Everyday Life: 1790-1840. New York. Harper & Row. 1988

Laws, Bill. Fifty Plants that Changed the Course of History. Richmond Hill, Ont. Firefly Books. 2010

McCullough, David. John Adams. NY. Simon & Schuster. 2001

Passoneau, Joseph. Washington Through Two Centuries. NY. Monacelli Press, Inc. 2004.

Robinson, David and Tanefis, Elizabeth. Post Card History Series – The Saco River. Columbus, S.C. Arcadia Publishing. 2010

Shepherd, Jack. The Adams Chronicles: Four Generations of Greatness. Boston. Little Brown & Company, 1975

Smith, David. A History of Lumbering in Maine: 1800-1860. Orono, ME. University of Maine Press. 1972

Washington, Booker T. Up from Slavery. Williamstown, MA. Corner House Publishers. 1971

Zanger, Mark H. The American History Cookbook. Westport, CT. Greenwood Press. 2003

Websites:

http://www.encyclopedia.com/topic/Panic_of_1819.aspx

htttp://en.wikipedia.org/wikicoinage_Act_of_1792

www.thehistorybox.com

http://www.merriam-webster.com/info/noah.htm

http://en.wikipedia.org/wiki/William_Wilberforce

www.eriecanal.org/

http://en.wikipedia.org/wiki/Crawford_Notch

www.whychristmas.com

http://www.sppurgeon.org.sermons/0057.htm

www.parkstreet.org/

http://en.wikipedia.org/wiki/Francis_Cabot_Lowell

http://www.mainememory/.net/sitebuilder/sit/760/
    page1169/display
www.wallbuilders.com
www.loc.gov/exhibits/religion/re106-2http

Interviews:

Interview with James Record, lifelong resident of North
    Fryeburg, by Doug and Paula Albert, current owners of
    the Benjamin Wiley House on May 21, 2013.

Book IV Journeys from Home

Fryeburg is no longer an isolated hamlet as world events impact the Miller family. Senator Benjamin Miller's grandson, Thaddeus Pierce, travels throughout Europe and the United States to cover stories for the New York Post. Hannah takes in a troubled ten-year old boy, orphaned by the potato famine in Ireland. Rachel Miller leaves home to work in a textile mill in Biddeford, befriending a Catholic, French Canadian immigrant.

Meanwhile in Fryeburg a tragic accident on the Saco River devastates the Miller family. Jacob and his son Eli organize an agricultural fair as Danny expands his saw mill. Grace is dismayed when she discovers the younger generation knows little about the history of their home town. After his beloved Fryeburg Academy burns to the ground, Benjamin devotes himself to the rebuilding of the school.

About the Author

June O'Donal, a "retired" homeschool mom, believes history is fascinating and relevant. Now the author of three books in the series of *The Fryeburg Chronicles*, she hopes students and adults alike will appreciate how international, national and local events can impact a family and understand how the decisions and actions of one generation impacts future generations. She has developed several power point presentations on different aspects of history and enjoys speaking to various organizations and homeschool events. Please visit *The Fryeburg Chronicles* Facebook page to view photos of her research, her husband's newly completed birch bark canoe and more.

Slavery did not end with the American Civil War. Today there are 27-30 million people enslaved in global human trafficking. To learn more please visit www.notforsalecampaign.org.